The CRT Controller Handbook

The CRT Controller Handbook

Gerry Kane

OSBORNE/McGraw-Hill
Berkeley, California

This book may be used to update Section H of *An Introduction to Microcomputers: Volume 3 — Some Real Support Devices*, Osborne/McGraw-Hill, 1978.

Published by
OSBORNE/McGraw-Hill
630 Bancroft Way
Berkeley, California 94710
U. S. A

For information on translations and book distributors outside of the U. S. A. , please write OSBORNE/McGraw-Hill at the above address.

THE CRT CONTROLLER HANDBOOK

1234567890 CPCP 89876543210

ISBN 0-931988-45-4

Technical reviews by: William Houghton, Intel Corporation; Richard Palm, Synertek Incorporated; Vincent Rende, Standard Microsystems Corporation; Charles Carinalli, National Semiconductor.

Technical edit by Patrick McGuire, Leland Research. Cover design by Marc Miyashiro.

Contents

1

CRT Principles of Operation

Cathode ray tubes (CRTs) are ubiquitous devices. Most homes have several in the form of TV sets, and CRT-based terminals are used widely in both data processing and word processing computer systems. The widespread and ever increasing use of CRTs in computer terminals has led semiconductor manufacturers to design large-scale-integrated (LSI) devices to simplify and reduce the costs of control functions for CRT-based terminals.

In this book we will describe a number of LSI CRT controller devices. Although there are significant differences between the functions, capabilities, and characteristics of each of these CRT controllers, all of them have been shaped by the requirements of the cathode ray tube itself and by prevailing interface standards to this device. In this chapter we will describe general principles of operation for the CRT and those terms and definitions which apply to all of the CRT controllers we will describe.

THE CATHODE RAY TUBE

The theory of operation of the cathode ray tube is described in great detail in numerous texts. Therefore, our description here will be quite simple; we will concern ourselves only with the general aspects of the theory which you should know in order to understand the interface between a CRT and its controller.

Figure 1-1 is a simplified representation of a CRT. A cathode ray tube is an evacuated glass tube which has a fluorescent coating on the inner surface of its rectangular frontal region (screen). An electron gun positioned at the end of the narrow cylindrical part of the tube (the neck) emits an electron beam. This stream of electrons strikes the fluorescent inner surface of the screen to produce an illuminated phosphor dot.

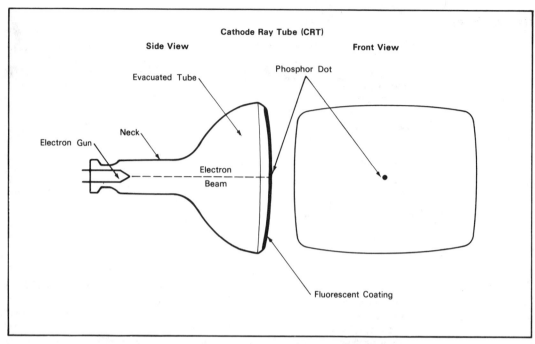

Figure 1-1. Simplified Representation of a Cathode Ray Tube (CRT)

You can control the point at which the electron beam strikes the screen, and therefore the position of the dot upon the screen, by deflecting the electron beam. There are two primary methods of performing this beam deflection: electromagnetic and electrostatic. Electromagnetic deflection is by far the more common method and is used in all conventional television sets. Separate deflection coils are provided along the horizontal and vertical axes of the CRT neck. **Separate signals** can then be applied to **effect horizontal and vertical deflection of the electron beam and thus move it across the surface of the screen. This operation is illustrated in Figure 1-2.**

Persistence **As the beam is moved across the screen, it leaves a trace which takes some finite amount of time to dissipate.** The duration of this trace depends on the characteristics of the fluorescent coating applied to the inner surface of the screen. This characteristic is called the "persistence" of the phosphor.

The horizontal deflection signal applied to the deflection coils affects only the horizontal position of the illuminated dot; likewise, the vertical deflection signal affects only its vertical position. Some CRT displays allow the user to arbitrarily position the dot by providing a horizontal and vertical input. With this type of display, the dot position is proportional to the linear voltages applied to these two inputs. **This type of display is often referred to as a graphic, X-Y, or vector CRT display.**

Raster Scan

The far more prevalent type of CRT display is called a raster scan type. This type is used in all modern commercial television sets and in most CRT terminals designed for the display of alphanumeric data. Within this type of display are generated the horizontal and vertical deflection signals to move the beam in a pattern illustrated as follows:

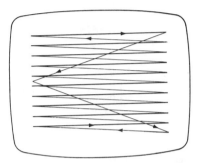

The raster scan pattern that we have illustrated still does not provide any method for displaying useful information on the CRT screen; so far, all we've done is produce a rake-like pattern on the screen. **The first step towards making the screen useful is to eliminate the retrace portion of the raster scan pattern.** This can be done by reducing the intensity of the electron beam during the retrace portion, using the intensity control for video input to the CRT illustrated in Figure 1-2. **If the intensity of the electron beam is sufficiently reduced during retrace, then the flourescent coating on the screen will not be sufficiently excited to produce an illuminated trace.** The resultant pattern on the screen can be illustrated as follows:

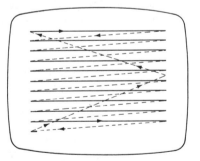

The dotted lines in this illustration represent the retrace portion of the raster scan pattern when the electron beam intensity is reduced. The dotted lines would not be visible to a viewer. Now we have a series of approximately 10 horizontal lines or traces that are continuously displayed on the screen. While this is some improvement over the zigzag pattern that included retrace lines, we are still not displaying any useful information.

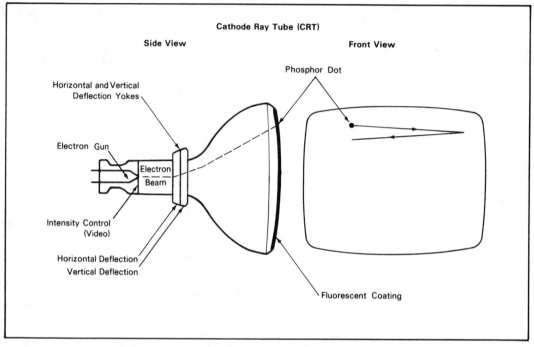

Figure 1-2. Controlling the Movement of the CRT Electron Beam

To see how information can be displayed on the screen, let us arbitrarily define our screen as having 10 horizontal traces or lines, and then let us divide each of those lines into seven segments. The resultant display could be represented as follows:

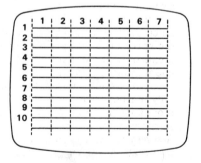

We are going to use this seven-by-ten (7 × 10) matrix of line segments to display a single alphanumeric character. To provide a separation border around this alphanumeric character, we will leave the top line and the bottom two lines blank and provide a one-segment border on the left and right edges of the 7 × 10 matrix. This border is provided by reducing the intensity of the electron beam during the appropriate segments of the scan pattern. **We**

will then be left with a 5 × 7 matrix of line segments or dots in the center of our field:

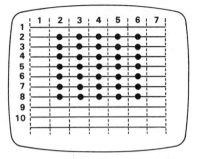

We can now represent alphanumeric characters within this 5 × 7 matrix by reducing the intensity of the electron beam during the appropriate line segments. For example, the letter "R" can be represented as follows:

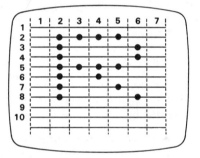

The beam intensity is reduced during the entire scan of line 1, during line segments 1, 6 and 7 of scan line 2, and so on. Thus, it would take seven consecutive scan lines to represent the letter R with a number of illuminated line segments or dots on each scan line representing part of the letter. Each illuminated dot will remain illuminated for some finite period of time depending on the persistence rating of the flourescent coating on the screen. The line segments or dots representing the character must be repeated or refreshed at frequent intervals, or the character will simply fade away.

In our discussion of the character formation using scan lines, we showed only ten horizontal lines. Obviously, a typical CRT screen can display many more lines than this, and each line will be subdivided into many more dots or segments than the few that we have illustrated. **Let us now discuss the factors involved in determining the number of scan lines and dots or segments per line that are commonly used.**

Horizontal and Vertical Scan Rates

In the United States, the horizontal sweep or scan rate of the electron beam for television is 15.75 kHz. If the beam is simultaneously moved vertically at a rate of 60 Hz, then 262.5 (15,750 ÷ 60) horizontal trace lines can be produced while the beam is moved from the top to the bottom of the screen. Of course, some time is required to accomplish the horizontal and vertical retrace operations. Thus, some of the scan lines are effectively lost while performing the vertical retrace. A typical video system might require 21 or 22 scan lines of time to perform the vertical retrace, leaving about 240 raster scan lines for display of data. If we used 10 scan lines to form each row of alphanumeric characters, we could get a total of 24 lines of characters on the screen.

The number of characters that you can display horizontally along one of the rows depends on the video frequency used; that is, the rate at which you modulate the intensity of the electron beam. For example, if the horizontal scan frequency is 15.75 kHz and you want to display 100 8-dot wide characters per line, you would need a video frequency of 12.6 MHz (15,750 × 8 × 100 = 12.6 MHz). In an actual system you would blank about 20% of these characters to allow for horizontal retrace time and side margins, and would thus have an 80-character per line display with this video frequency.

The number of lines of data that can be displayed on the screen can be increased in several ways. The most obvious way would be to increase the horizontal sweep frequency so that more horizontal scan lines are produced during vertical scan of the screen. For example, if we increased the horizontal scan frequency from 15.75 kHz to 18 kHz and kept the vertical frequency at 60 Hz, we would increase the number of horizontal scan lines from 252.5 to 300 (18,000 ÷ 60 = 300). However, increasing the horizontal frequency may mean that you must use nonstandard beam deflection components to achieve this higher sweep or scan rate. In addition, you must now also increase the video frequency if you still wish to attain the same number of characters per line. Thus this approach to increasing the number of data rows can be quite expensive.

Refresh Frequency

Another approach is to reduce the vertical scan frequency. For example, if you maintained the horizontal frequency at 15.75 kHz but decreased the vertical frequency from 60 Hz to 45 Hz, you would increase the number of horizontal scan lines from 262.5 to 350 (15,750 ÷ 45 = 350). The main problem with this approach to increasing the number of scan lines is that if the vertical refresh rate is not synchronized with the CRT's power line frequency, the electron beam can be deflected by stray magnetic fields, especially those produced by nearby power transformers. This effect can cause raster jitters if the sources of magnetic interference are not adequately shielded. For this reason it is usually advisable to have the refresh frequency be the same as the power line frequency. Therefore, the refresh frequency used in the United States is usually 60 Hz, while in other countries where the power frequency is 50 Hz the refresh frequency for CRTs is usually 50 Hz.

**Interlaced
Scanning**

Another method of increasing the number of scan lines available for displaying data is to use a method known as interlaced scan. This is the scanning method used in broadcast television. In an interlaced scanning system, only half of the screen is refreshed during each vertical sweep cycle. Interlaced scanning can be illustrated as follows:

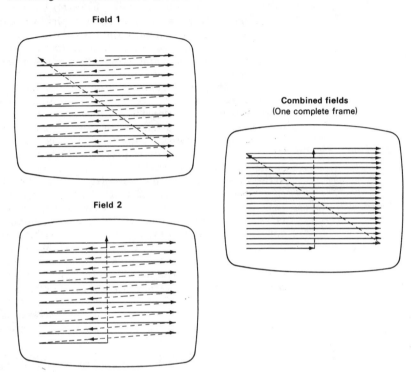

Field 1

Combined fields
(One complete frame)

Field 2

An interlaced raster scanning system employs two sweep fields: when the electron beam reaches the middle of the first field's bottom line (line 262 in the illustration) it retraces not back to the top left corner, but rather to the middle of the top line where it is offset vertically by half a line. Thus the first line (line 263) of the second field is traced between the first two lines (lines 1 and 2) of the first field. The fields combine to make up one complete display frame.

One of the problems with this interlaced scan method is that you effectively halve the refresh rate: if the vertical sweep frequency is 60 Hz then a particular line on the screen will only be refreshed at a 30 Hz frequency. This 525 lines per frame, 262.5 lines per field interlaced scanning pattern we have just described is the system that is used in the United States for broadcast television. Since television scene content consists of large white areas, with adjacent fields being repeated, the low refresh rate provided in the interlaced scan method is quite acceptable. However, if you are using the CRT to display alphanumeric characters, all of the displayed data consists of small elements, and adjacent elements are not the same. In this application, an annoying flicker will usually result at a 30 Hz refresh rate unless a long persistence phosphor is used on the CRT screen.

THE CRT CONTROLLER-CRT MONITOR INTERFACE

A typical low-cost CRT monitor provides three signal connections to a CRT controller and associated electronics. The three signals are Horizontal Syncronization (HSYNC), Vertical Synchronization (VSYNC), and VIDEO. These signals are applied to the CRT monitor's electronics, and the horizontal and vertical deflection as was illustrated in Figure 1-2 are generated internally and applied to the CRT itself.

The horizontal and vertical sweep oscillators of a CRT monitor are free running, and scanning is usually continuous; the purpose of the synchronization signals is not to start or stop the scan motion, but rather to shorten or lengthen the existing scan motions so that you can synchronize the presentation of information via the electron beam. The intensity of the electron beam is modulated by the video input to the CRT monitor. Commercial TV sets usually include video amplifier circuitry which can provid gray levels by properly regulating the beam intensity. In CRT monitors intended for display of alphanumeric data, however, simple on/off or black-white levels are all that are necessary to produce dots or no dots. Blanking levels are also fed to the video input to turn off the electron beam for the return trip or retrace on each horizontal scan and vertical frame scan.

Composite Video
On some CRT monitors, a single input signal called "composite video" is provided. The composite video signal includes HSYNC, VSYNC, and VIDEO. The CRT monitor then provides the circuitry to separate out the three signals comprising the composite video input. The major advantage of a composite video signal over three separate input signals is that this composite signal can be sent with a single coaxial cable. This is more convenient over long cable runs or in systems where the video display must be switched from one source to another.

CRT CHARACTER GENERATOR LOGIC

In our preceding discussion of the CRT monitor, we briefly described how a single character can be created on the CRT screen. A series of dots is "painted" on the screen on successive scan lines to form a single character. The dot information is input to the CRT monitor serially on the VIDEO input. Obviously, some logic must be provided to convert data that is normally handled in 8-bit parallel bytes in a microcomputer system into the serial bit stream needed to create a corresponding data character on the CRT screen. In addition, since each character on the screen is represented by many dots, it will take more than eight bits of information to represent an alphanumeric character. Lastly, we will want to be able to write more than one character on a line; this implies that some sort of buffering will be required. Let us begin by seeing what would be needed to generate the characters for a single 80-character row on the CRT screen.

Figure 1-3 illustrates the sequence that occurs when displaying a single 80-character row of alphanumeric data on a CRT screen. First, the dot information for scan line 1 is applied via the VIDEO input to the CRT.

The dot pattern for all 80 characters on scan line 1 must be presented consecutively. When the first scan line is completed, the dot information for scan line 2 must be presented to the CRT. Once again, the dot information for all 80 characters must be applied consecutively. This sequence is repeated until all of the scan lines (seven in our illustration) for that character row have been

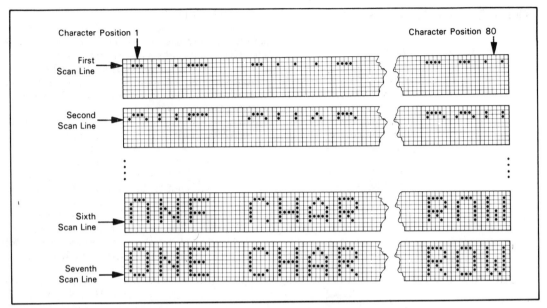

Figure 1-3. Display of One 80-Character Row of Data

completed. Thus dot information for each of the 80 characters on the character row must be presented to the CRT a total of seven times. The dot pattern presented for each character differs for every scan line. To see how the dot information for each character could be provided, let us examine the composition of a single character.

In Figure 1-3, each character is created in a 5 × 7 matrix. Thus each character is actually represented by a total of 35 dots which can be either on or off. We could therefore store the pattern for a single character in a 35-bit memory device which could be represented as follows:

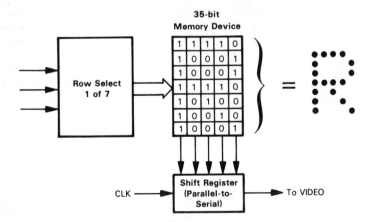

Now, with three row-select inputs to this read-only memory (ROM) device, we can select the dot patterns for each of the seven rows of the character. As each dot row pattern for the character is read out of this ROM, it can be loaded into a shift register and then sent serially to the VIDEO input of the CRT. **That takes care of one character, but we must consecutively provide the dot pattern for each of the 80 characters on a character row. Obviously, we need a larger memory storage element.**

If we want to be able to represent a standard 64-character set, with each character represented by a 5 × 7-dot pattern, we will need a 2240-bit memory device (64 × 7 × 5 = 2240). This device could be represented as follows:

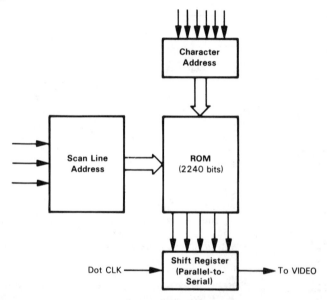

We could now address the desired character in this ROM using six address inputs, and specify the dot row of that character using the three row select or scan line address inputs. As each character is required for presentation to the CRT, the character address inputs are changed to select the necessary character, while the scan line address inputs to the device access the correct dot pattern for the current scan line.

There are two problems with the simple approach we have illustrated: we are using an unnecessarily large number of address lines, and we have not defined a way in which we can consecutively present the proper character addresses to the ROM device. The first problem is easily dealt with: since we will always be accessing the scan lines in consecutive order (1 through 7) **we can simply provide a scan line counter which will increment the scan line address (or dot row address) to the ROM as each CRT scan line is completed.** In our illustrated example, a three-bit counter could be used to generate the scan line addresses:

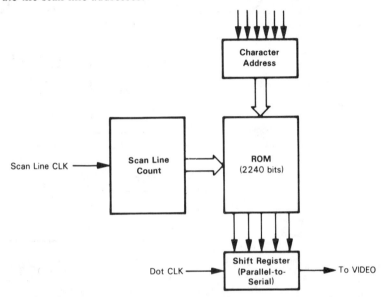

Now the scan line address inputs to the ROM will remain constant for a complete scan line, while the character address inputs will be changed to address the dot pattern for each of the characters on an 80-character row. When a scan line is completed, the counter is incremented to select the next dot pattern row and the same 80-character sequence will be repeated until all seven rows have been scanned. When a subsequent 80-character row is to be presented to the CRT, the 3-bit row counter will be reset to once again address dot row 1 for the new character sequence.

Character Generators

The ROM, scan line address counter, and parallel-to-serial shifter logic that we have just described comprise what we call a character generator. Because this combination of devices is used so frequently, a number of companies provide fully integrated character generator devices. You can get character generator devices that provide the required dot patterns for full ASCII character sets with a 5 × 7 or 7 × 9-dot matrix for each character. **The amount of logic included on character generator devices varies:** some include character address latches, scan line counters, and parallel-to-serial shifters, while other character generators may consist simply of the ROM with the required dot patterns stored in the device. **For purposes of our discussion, we will define the character generator functions as including the elements illustrated below:**

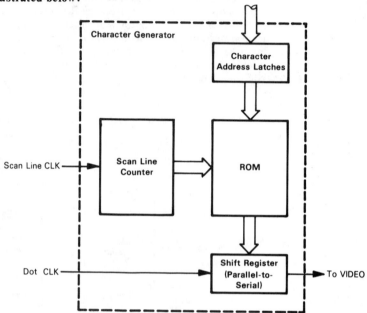

Now that we are familiar with the character generator functions, **we must still find a way to successively present the character address inputs to the character generator and to present this 80-character sequence of addresses repetitively (once for each scan line) as each character row on the CRT is written. One simple scheme would be to construct an 80-character buffer which would be loaded with the data that is to be displayed.** The characters in this buffer would then be accessed one after the other and presented to the character generator as each scan line is written to the CRT. The contents of this 80-character buffer would be accessed once for each scan line comprising a character row (seven times in our 5 × 7 matrix example). **The relationship between the character row buffer and the character generator can be illustrated as follows:**

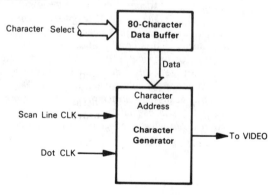

One aspect of this relationship may not be obvious: the data word from the 80-character buffer is used as an address input to the character generator. Although the use of a data word as an address may seem a bit unusual, there is no reason why the bit pattern representing a character cannot be used as an address; each character has a unique bit pattern and thus presents a unique address to the character generator ROM.

SCREEN MEMORY

Thus far, we have developed the logic necessary to present one 80-character row of data to the CRT for display. You will recall, however, that data on the CRT screen must be refreshed or rewritten to the screen at frequent intervals (50 or 60 Hz). In addition, the screen will be comprised of more than a single line of characters. One solution is to set aside an entire block of memory for storage of data that is to be displayed on the screen. For example, if our CRT screen is going to be capable of displaying twenty-four 80-character lines of information, we can assign a block of 1920 (80 × 24) memory locations to store the screen data.

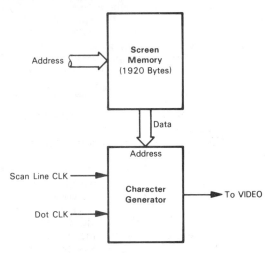

Screen
Memory

The memory used to store the data for display on the screen is referred to as screen memory. The data in the screen memory is presented to the character generator, which then sends the appropriate dot stream to the CRT. Logic must be provided to address the screen memory so that the appropriate data will be accessed for presentation to the character generator. The data in the screen memory could be accessed as 80-byte lines, with each of the twenty-four 80-byte lines accessed seven times in order to produce the seven scan lines that comprise a character row. The preceding illustration shows data from screen memory being applied directly to the character generator. However, we have not provided a path for putting data into screen memory; obviously, screen memory would not be read-only memory, since we want to be able to vary the data that is displayed on the CRT screen. Typically, screen memory would simply be connected to the system data bus as shown in the following illustration:

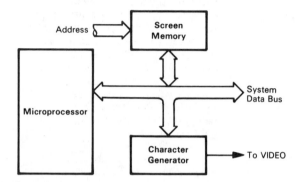

Now the microprocessor can load screen memory with data that is to be displayed on the CRT screen. Subsequently, the stored data in screen memory can be applied to the character generator as required to create the display. One problem with this arrangement is that the character generator requires that the same data be applied to it over and over again in order to create the dot stream for the CRT. This results in the system data bus being used almost continuously to pass data from screen memory to the character generator. Use of the system data bus for this purpose could be greatly reduced by combining the 80-character line buffer which we discussed earlier with the screen memory approach:

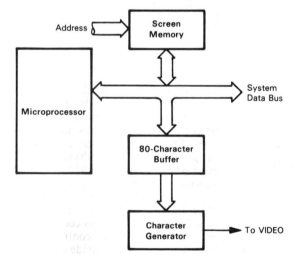

A complete character row can now be loaded into this buffer from screen memory via the system data bus. The contents of the 80-character buffer will then be repeatedly presented to the character generator while the scan lines comprising a character row are being sent to the CRT screen. With this approach, the system data bus will be used by the CRT-related devices only when a new line of characters must be passed from screen memory into the line buffer. While use of the system data bus by CRT-related functions is still significant, the line buffer approach does help to alleviate traffic.

The preceding illustration still does not deal with the logic required to generate the addresses to access screen memory; this is one of the functions typically provided by a CRT controller. The following illustration includes a logic block to generate addresses for screen memory:

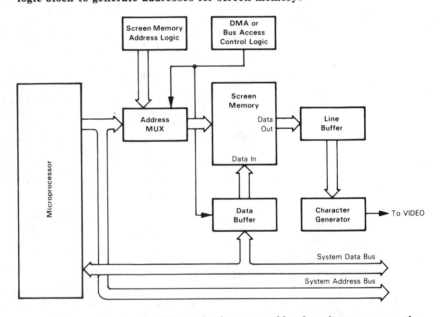

Since screen memory must also be accessed by the microprocessor, the preceding figure includes address multiplexing logic and data buffering logic. There are, however, a number of other techniques that might be used to provide for bus sharing by the CRT-related devices and the microprocessor. The method used in a particular system depends on the various system demands as well as on the characteristics of the CRT controller being used. For example, Intel's 8275 CRT controller usually requires the use of an external DMA controller in the system. Other CRT controllers provide some minimal bus access contention logic to simplify coordination of system bus sharing. Some CRT controllers provide no DMA or bus access contention logic, and you must provide all the necessary logic externally.

MANIPULATION OF CRT SCREEN DATA

Cursor

We have seen how a copy of the data that is to be displayed on a CRT screen is maintained in screen memory. When you want to change information that is displayed on the screen, you simply write the new information into screen memory at the appropriate location. **When a CRT display is being used as part of a terminal, some method must be provided so that an operator can determine and control the location on the CRT screen where new data is to be entered. Therefore, all of the CRT controllers we will describe can generate and display a cursor on the screen. The cursor is simply a visible symbol that may be moved about the screen where a transaction is to take place. The cursor is typically displayed as a horizontal line below a character position:**

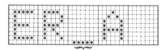

Underscore cursor

Some of the CRT controllers allow you to program the cursor so that it appears as a block rather than as a single line. The cursor can also be made to automatically blink on and off with some CRT controllers. **A block-type cursor symbol can be illustrated as follows:**

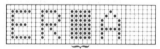

Block cursor

Light Pen Inputs

The primary method used to coordinate the input of data by an operator to an appropriate spot on the CRT screen is to position a cursor to indicate the point of entry. **An alternate method, often used in graphic-oriented CRT systems, is a light pen input.** With this method, you simply hold the light pen against the CRT screen to physically indicate the position where a transaction or change is to occur. Implementing a light pen input into a CRT system requires additional external hardware and implies the presence of some additional logic. To understand what is required, let us briefly discuss how the light pen input works.

Light pens are actually light sensor devices. When you hold the light pen against the CRT screen, it will detect the passage of the CRT's electron beam in front of the pen, generating a pulse which is sent to the CRT controller. Since the CRT controller is generating all of the scan line and character counts for the CRT screen, it knows the position of the electron beam on the screen at any given moment. Thus, when it receives the signal from the light pen, the values from the controller's appropriate counting registers can be saved to record the position of the light pen.

Several of the CRT controller devices we will describe provide a light pen input. All of them simply use an internal register to store the appropriate counter values at the time when the light pen input signal is received. The microprocessor can then read the value stored in the register to determine the location of the light pen.

Scrolling　　　　If the CRT screen is being used for entry of data or display of text, it is often desirable to make the screen appear as though it were a sheet of paper in a typewriter. Text is entered beginning at the top line of the screen and subsequent lines are entered below. When the bottom line of the screen is reached, the text on the screen is moved up, or scrolled. Scrolling on the screen causes the top line to be lost from view while creating a vacant bottom line for entry of additional data. This scrolling operation can be illustrated as follows:

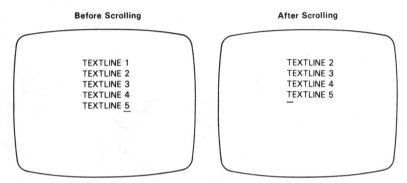

There are a number of ways that the scrolling operation can be implemented. The most straightforward method from a conceptual point of view is to simply move the data in screen memory. This approach can be illustrated as follows:

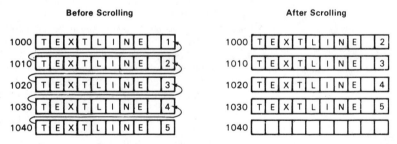

There is a very obvious problem with this approach: moving all of the data around in screen memory requires an unacceptably large amount of time and attention from the microprocessor.

A much simpler method of performing the scrolling function is to maintain a register which will hold the screen memory address where the first line of displayed data begins. This address, which we will call TOP, would be used as the starting point when screen memory is accessed at the beginning of the first scan line on the screen. When the contents of the screen are to be scrolled upwards, the register holding the TOP address is incremented by a value corresponding to the number of characters contained in one line. This approach can be illustrated as follows:

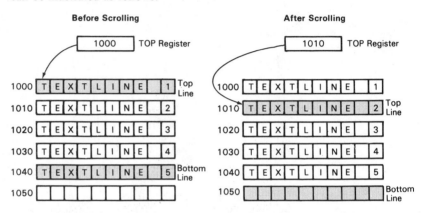

With this approach, no actual movement of data is required. We have simply changed the starting location of screen memory and thus effectively moved the data that is displayed on the screen upward. Using this approach, you could also scroll downward since the previous top line (TEXTLINE 1) is still available in memory beginning at location 1000.

The scrolling operations we have thus far illustrated moved data one line at a time. There is no reason, however, why we could not scroll the screen data on a character-by-character basis if we desired. For example, we could scroll the screen data four characters upwards and to the left by adding 4 to the TOP register value as follows:

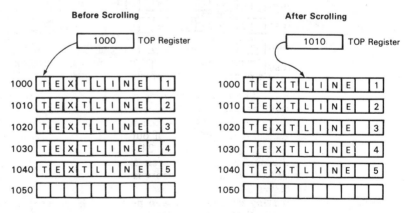

The display that would result from this type of character scrolling operation can be illustrated as follows:

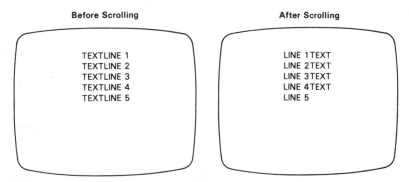

Before Scrolling

TEXTLINE 1
TEXTLINE 2
TEXTLINE 3
TEXTLINE 4
TEXTLINE 5

After Scrolling

LINE 1 TEXT
LINE 2 TEXT
LINE 3 TEXT
LINE 4 TEXT
LINE 5

Scrolling by manipulation of the contents of the screen memory starting address greatly reduces the burden placed on the microprocessor since no actual movement of data is required. You will note, however, that this scrolling technique still requires that memory locations being "scrolled into view" be cleared or loaded with the value representing a space character. For example, in the following line scrolling operation you must be sure that the ten screen memory locations beginning at location 1050 are cleared, since whatever is contained in those locations will be displayed as the bottom line on the screen after scrolling.

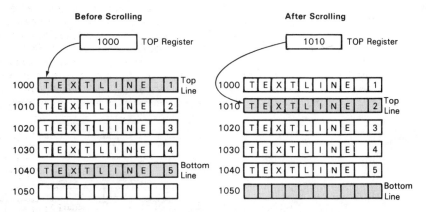

Before Scrolling

After Scrolling

There is one obvious problem with the type of scrolling operation we have been illustrating. Each time we scroll, we effectively move a "window," whose size is equal to the display capacity of the screen, through memory. For example, if our screen displays 24 80-character lines, then we must provide 1920 (80 × 24) bytes of screen memory. Each time that we scroll the display, we require an additional 80 bytes of memory, as the starting address for screen memory is incremented by 80. After we have scrolled the screen 24 times we will have utilized 3840 (1920 × 2) memory locations. **This moving window of screen memory will be unacceptable in many applications. Fortunately, there is a simple solution.** To illustrate these solutions, let's assume that our screen consists of eight 16-character lines. We therefore need 128 bytes of screen memory which we will position at addresses 1000_{16} through $107F_{16}$. Now, when the entire screen is filled with text and we want to scroll the screen data upward, we must add 16_{16} (10_{10}) to the TOP register. This can be illustrated as follows:

Before Scrolling

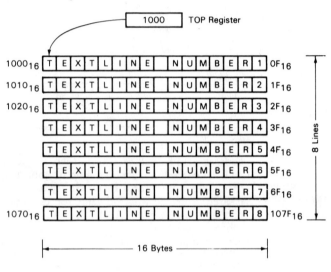

After Scrolling

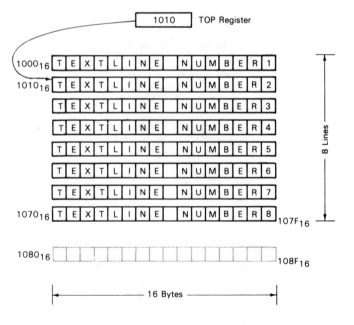

When the next scan of screen memory begins, it will now start with location 1010_{16}. Eight lines of text (128 characters) will be displayed; however, the bottom line displayed on the screen will not consist of the contents of memory locations 1080_{16} through $108F_{16}$; instead, TEXTLINE NUMBER1 from memory locations 1000_{16} through $100F_{16}$ will be displayed as the bottom line. The screen display can be illustrated as follows:

```
┌──────────────────────────┐   ┌──────────────────────────┐
│                          │   │                          │
│   TEXTLINE NUMBER 1      │   │      TEXTLINE NUMBER2    │
│   TEXTLINE NUMBER 2      │   │      TEXTLINE NUMBER3    │
│   TEXTLINE NUMBER 3      │   │      TEXTLINE NUMBER4    │
│   TEXTLINE NUMBER 4      │   │      TEXTLINE NUMBER5    │
│   TEXTLINE NUMBER 5      │   │      TEXTLINE NUMBER6    │
│   TEXTLINE NUMBER 6      │   │      TEXTLINE NUMBER7    │
│   TEXTLINE NUMBER 7      │   │      TEXTLINE NUMBER8    │
│   TEXTLINE NUMBER 8      │   │      TEXTLINE NUMBER1    │
│                          │   │                          │
└──────────────────────────┘   └──────────────────────────┘
```

Memory Wraparound

This phenomenon is due to wraparound of screen memory. In our example we require only 128 bytes of screen memory. Only seven address lines (A0-A6) are required to select one of the 128 locations. Therefore, the screen memory addressing logic need only generate seven address signals for connection to the screen memory. When the last character in the last row of screen memory (location $107F_{16}$) is being accessed, the seven address signals generated by the screen memory address logic will all be set to 1 to represent the address $7F_{16}$. The next time the screen memory address logic is incremented, the seven address lines will all be set low. Since only these seven address lines need be applied to the screen memory to select one of the 128 locations, the next location that will be accessed after $107F_{16}$ will be the first location in screen memory (1000_{16}). The more significant address lines needed to represent the address 1080_{16} are not connected to screen memory and are therefore not a factor in the screen function. They may, of course, be used in other ways within a system to select other memory or I/O devices, or as chip enable inputs to the screen memory devices, but these uses can be made transparent so far as the screen memory address logic is concerned.

There is still one problem with this wraparound technique of scrolling. In the example we just illustrated, all of the text has been moved up one line. However, since the last line of screen memory now effectively consists of memory locations 00_{16} through $0F_{16}$, the bottom line of the screen will display TEXTLINE NUMBER1. In order to have the last line of the display cleared, the microprocessor must write blanks or spaces into the appropriate line of screen memory. In addition, the line of screen memory that must be cleared will change with each scrolling operation. For example, after the bottom line of screen memory has been cleared and a new text line (TEXTLINE NUMBER9) has been entered, the following scrolling procedure would be performed:

Before Scrolling

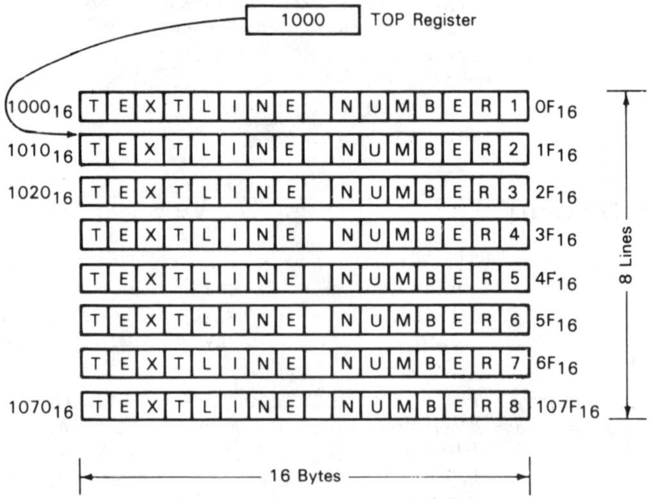

After Scrolling

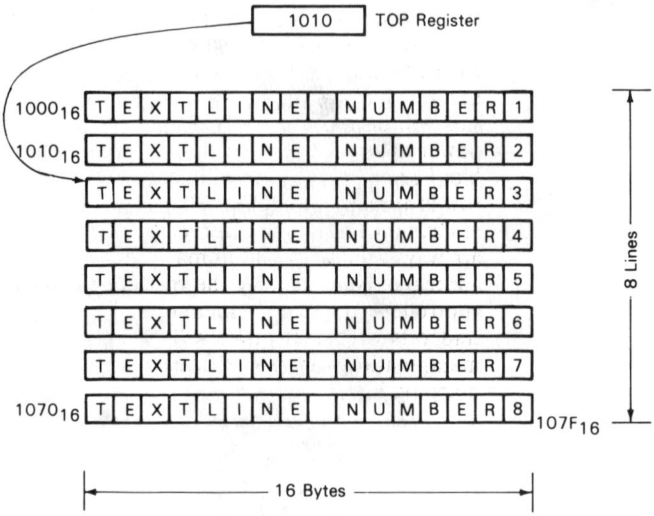

Now the top of screen memory begins at address 1020_{16}, and it is the old TEXTLINE NUMBER2, which begins at screen memory location 1010_{16}, that must be cleared by the microprocessor to clear the bottom line displayed on the screen. This scrolling procedure obviously imposes some burden on the microprocessor to keep track of the current bottom line of display memory and clear that line as part of each scrolling operation. However, this wraparound approach to scrolling makes the screen memory address logic provided by a CRT controller quite straightforward. And, since it is this addressing logic which makes the majority of accesses to screen memory, it is important that this logic be kept simple.

Screen Memory Addressing: Linear versus Row/Column

In our preceding discussion of screen memory addressing, we assumed that memory is addressed linearly; that is, the addressing is done as though all locations on the display were stored in a continuous string of memory locations. This is the way that microprocessors assume that memory is configured. This approach is not always the most efficient, however. For example, if you are manipulating the data that is displayed on a CRT screen, it is often most convenient and efficient if the data can be handled on a display line basis. This is especially true when you want to implement text editing functions such as insert line, delete line, and insert/delete character. Therefore, some of the CRT controllers provide screen memory addressing on a row/column basis. In this approach, some of the memory address lines specify the data row of the character. While this approach can simplify the software required to perform many data manipulation functions on the CRT screen, it is accomplished at the cost of memory usage efficiency. To illustrate this, consider the figure below.

As you can see, using standard linear addressing, the first character on each row is simply stored in the next consecutive memory location following the last character on the preceding row. If row/column addressing is used, then this will be the case only if the number of characters on a row equals some power of two. Otherwise, some memory locations will effectively be inaccessible. For example, in the illustration above, the last character on the first data row is at memory address 80_{10} while the first character on the next data row is at location 128_{10}. The intervening memory addresses are not accessible. There are ways around the dilemma, such as using external logic or ROM to map the addresses generated by the microprocessor and those generated by the CRT controller for screen memory into the same address spaces. Thus, the tradeoffs you must make will be between more complicated software for text manipulation versus inefficient use of memory space and additional address mapping logic.

Linear (Binary) Addressing (Decimal addresses)

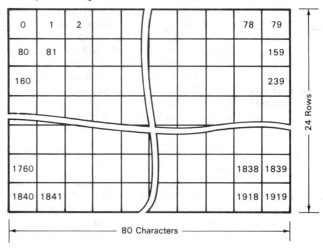

Row/Column Addressing (Decimal addresses)

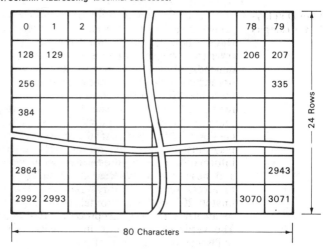

Memory Contention Logic

Although there are a number of methods that can be used to resolve screen memory contention existing between the microprocessor and the CRT controller, there are three techniques that are most commonly used: direct memory access (DMA), interlaced memory access, and, for want of a better term, what we will call non-display-time access.

Direct Memory Access

The DMA approach utilizes an external DMA controller to handle transfers of data between the microprocessor and screen memory, and between screen memory and the CRT controller. With this technique, the CRT controller will not always have access to screen memory. Instead, blocks of data, typically one character line, will be transferred under control of the DMA controller from screen memory to the CRT controller logic. This approach is the one used in the Intel 8275 CRT controller which provides two 80-character buffers to hold data from screen memory.

Interlaced Memory Access

The interlaced memory technique assumes that the CRT controller and microprocessor will have equal and alternating periods of time when they can access screen memory. For example, the 6800 and 6500 families of microprocessors use two-phase clocks, and the microprocessor will only be using the system busses during one of the two phases. Therefore, the CRT controller can be guaranteed access to the busses during the alternate phases. We will discuss this technique in more detail when we describe the 6845 and 6545 CRT controllers.

Non-Display-Time Access

A third technique for resolving screen memory contention consists of granting the microprocessor access to screen memory during non-display times when the CRT controller logic does not need access. The amount of time that will be available to the microprocessor to access screen memory depends, of course, on your system design. For example, if the system does not include a line buffer between screen memory and the character generator, then the CRT controller will need almost continuous access to the screen memory. Even in this case, however, there are periods of time when screen memory can be accessed by the microprocessor. You will recall from our discussion of CRT timing that dot information for the alphanumeric character display must be presented during each horizontal scan line. However, no dot information need be presented during horizontal retrace or vertical retrace, and these time intervals can therefore be made available to the microprocessor to access screen memory. Typically, horizontal retrace represents approximately 20% of the horizontal scan line time; thus, 10-15 microseconds would be available to the microprocessor during each horizontal retrace operation. The vertical retrace time in a typical system would provide another 1-1.5 milliseconds at the end of each frame. Additionally, the contents of screen memory need not be applied to the character generator for every horizontal scan line: for example, a 5×7 dot matrix character might be centered in a 7×9 matrix. In this case, dot information would only be presented during seven of the nine scan lines which comprise a character row. Screen memory could therefore be made available to the microprocessor during the first and last scan lines of each character row.

Determining when screen memory can be accessed by the microprocessor will require some logic. However, this logic can be minimal since some of the useful signals such as vertical blanking and scan line counts will already be available in the system.

THE CRT TIMING CHAIN

Now that we have discussed the general characteristics of a CRT display, let us look a little more closely at the timing required. Since the North American broadcast standard for television requires a horizontal synchronization (HSYNC) pulse frequency of 15.75 kHz, the deflection components of most CRT monitors are designed to operate at that frequency +5-10%. Another limiting parameter of the CRT monitors is their video response; that is, the rate at which the electron beam can be modulated. The video response range is usually much wider and therefore less limiting than the horizontal synchronization requirements. We will therefore begin our discussion of CRT timing with the horizontal synchronization requirements.

HSYNC In the discussion that follows, you must keep in mind that the numerical values we will use, while realistic, were chosen to clarify the explanation. The actual values used will of course depend on the application and your particular requirements.

We are going to use a horizontal synchronization frequency of 15.625 kHz in our example. With this frequency, each horizontal scan line will be 64 microseconds in duration ($1 \div 15,625 = 64 \times 10^{-6}$). The HSYNC pulse is applied to the CRT monitor electronics near the end of each horizontal scan line. Part of the 64 microseconds available for each horizontal scan line must be used for application of the HSYNC pulse and for horizontal retrace time. In a typical CRT, approximately 20% of the total horizontal scan time must be used for retrace. The relationship between the display portion of a scan line, the HSYNC pulse and retrace time can be illustrated as follows:

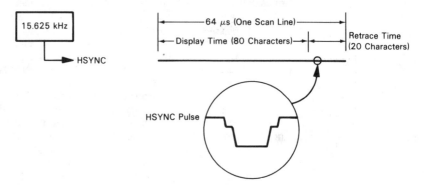

Before continuing with our description of the timing chain, let us look a bit more closely at the HSYNC signal. The horizontal retrace time can be subdivided into three intervals: the HSYNC delay, the HSYNC pulse, and the horizontal scan delay. This can be illustrated as follows:

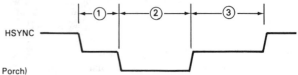

① HSYNC Delay (Front Porch)

② HSYNC Pulse

③ Horizontal Scan Delay (Back Porch)

**Front
Porch**

**Back
Porch**

The HSYNC delay is often referred to in television literature as the ''front porch,'' while the horizontal scan delay is frequently referred to as the ''back porch.'' The values for these three intervals will be determined by the operating characteristics of the CRT monitor you are using. Typical values for commercial CRT monitors would call for a total retrace time in the range of 10 to 12 microseconds and a ratio of HSYNC delay to HSYNC pulse to horizontal scan delay of 1:2:2. Thus, if we were allowing a total of 20 character times for horizontal retrace, the HSYNC delay (or front porch) would be 4 character times in duration, and the horizontal scan delay (back porch) would be 8 character times in duration. Now let us continue with our discussion of the timing chain.

If we want to display 80 characters per line, then we must divide the available horizontal scan time into approximately 100 character-times to allow for the 20% retrace requirement. Thus the horizontal scan time for each character along a line would be 640 nanoseconds ($64 \times 10^{-6} \div 100 = 640 \times 10^{-9}$). **Therefore, 640 nanoseconds of each horizontal scan line are required for each character that is to be formed. This can be illustrated as follows:**

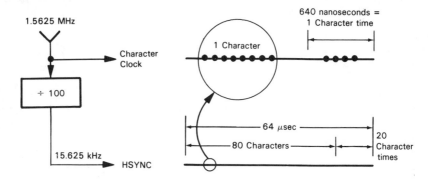

Character Clock

The 15.625 kHz frequency must be multiplied by 100 to derive the time allotted to a single character. Thus, the character clock frequency for our timing chain would be 1.5625 MHz.

We are going to use a 6 × 8 character formed in an 8 × 10 matrix for this example. Each character time along the horizontal scan line must therefore be divided into 8 dot times:

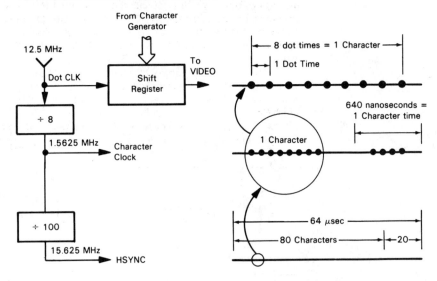

Dot Clock   The dot clock that we need to clock the shift register which generates VIDEO must therefore operate at a frequency of 12.5 MHz ($1.5625 \times 10^6 \times 8 = 12.5 \times 10^6$). This dot clock frequency is the highest that will be required in our system.

Now we have developed the timing chain from the highest frequency required down to the standard HSYNC frequency accepted by most CRT monitors. Since we have decided to use an 8×10 matrix to create each character on the screen, each character row will therefore require a total of 10 scan lines, or 640 microseconds including horizontal retrace time. A character or data row clock would thus run at a frequency of 1.562 kHz (15.625 kHz $\div$ 10).

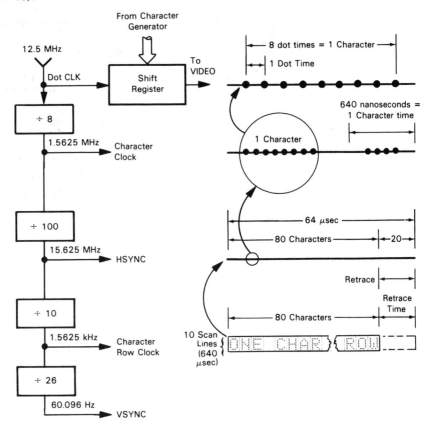

VSYNC　　　　　The next timing constraint we must deal with is the vertical synchronization (VSYNC) pulse used to initiate vertical retrace. You will recall that most CRT monitors in the U.S. are designed to operate with a VSYNC pulse frequency of 60 Hz. We could meet this parameter if the total number of horizontal scan lines on our screen was approximately 260 (15,625 ÷ 260 = 60.096). Thus, our display would consist of 26 character rows of 10 lines each. Of course, some time will be required for the vertical retrace operation. A typical value for this vertical retrace time might be 1 millisecond. So a period of time equivalent to 20 horizontal scan lines would give sufficient time (20 × 64 × 10⁻⁶ = 1.28 × 10⁻³) for the vertical retrace. This would leave a total of 240 scan lines, or 24 character rows for display of data.

Figure 1-4 illustrates the entire timing chain that we have developed. As we mentioned at the outset, the values we have used in this example were chosen for reasons of clarity. The actual values you use will doubtless be different. To highlight some of the ways in which you can vary the timing chain, let us simplify Figure 1-4 as follows:

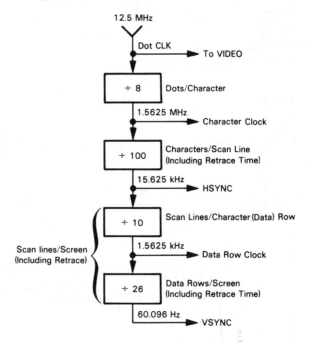

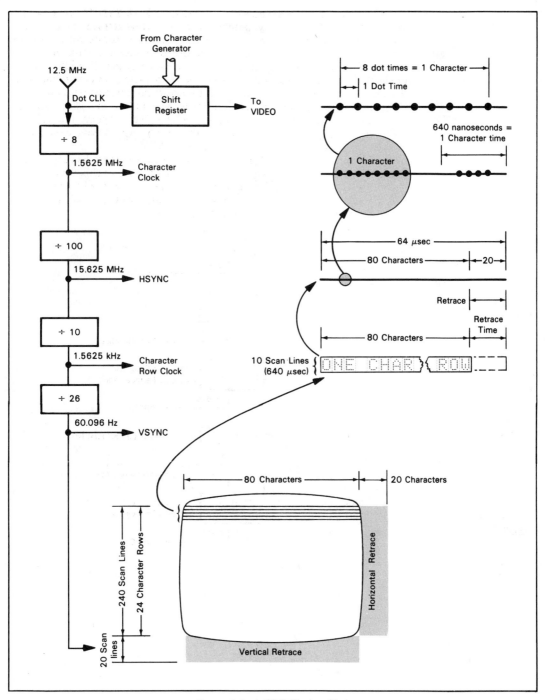

Figure 1-4. A CRT Timing Chain

In most applications, you will want to maintain a VSYNC frequency of 60 Hz and an HSYNC frequency that is near the commercial broadcast frequency of 15.75 kHz. Even with these constraints, however, there are still many changes we can make. For example, if we need to increase the number of characters that can be displayed on the screen we might develop the following timing chain:

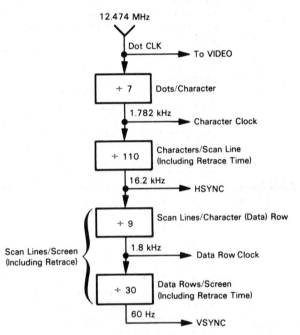

In this illustration, we have increased the number of characters per line and data rows per screen by using smaller characters: 5×7 characters in a 7×9 matrix instead of the 8×10 matrix of our first example. This results in a dot clock frequency that is slightly lower than that developed in our first example, and an HYSNC frequency that is somewhat higher than our previously chosen value. The HYSNC frequency is still close enough to the 15.75 kHz standard to be used with most CRT monitors, however.

GRAPHIC VERSUS ALPHANUMERIC DISPLAYS

Most of the CRT controllers we will describe are oriented towards alphanumeric displays where data comprising a character line is repetitively presented to character generator logic until all the scan lines comprising that character row have been displayed. With this arrangement, memory storage requirements and memory accesses are minimized and the character generator logic assumes responsibility for producing each individual dot required along a scan line.

By delegating responsibility for generating each dot on the CRT screen, you have also surrendered control of each dot and are limited in what you can display by the capabilities of the character generator logic. If you wish to display graphic information in which you must have the capability of individually manipulating every dot on the CRT screen, then a different approach is required. Typically, this different approach will consume more memory and may require additional resources beyond those usually provided by a CRT controller. The concept, however, is rather straightforward. Nonetheless, we will limit our discussion of this approach since the more widespread use of the CRT controllers we describe will be in alphanumeric display applications.

Bit-Mapped Screen Memory The most straightforward way of independently controlling every dot on the CRT screen is to map every dot to a specific memory data bit. Assuming that memory is organized as 8-bit bytes of data, you can store the dot information for eight dot locations on a scan line as one byte of memory. Thus, if the video portion of a scan line in an alphanumeric display application were used to present 80 characters, with each of them occupying seven dots along the scan line, then we could store the dot information for the scan line in 70 bytes of memory. Each 8-bit byte would be accessed from memory, loaded into a parallel-to-serial shift register, and then shifted serially at the dot clock frequency to create the CRT monitor video signal.

The memory storage requirements for a single scan line of individual dot information have not been increased beyond those required by alphanumeric data. However, while the same data stored in memory would be accessed repetitively for the 7-10 scan lines that might comprise a character row, the data for every scan line in a graphic application is unique and requires its own separate memory storage locations. If the CRT screen is to display 240 scan lines, then you must provide memory storage for 240 lines worth of dot information. In an alphanumeric application where each character row was comprised of 10 scan lines, you would only have to store 24 lines worth of data in memory.

Table 1-1 lists the CRT controller devices we will describe in this book and tabulates their salient functional capabilities.

Table 1-1. A Summary of CRT Controller Functional Characteristics

	Chapter 2	Chapter 3	Chapter 4	Chapter 5	Chapter 6
	DP8350 National Semiconductor	8275 Intel	6845 Motorola	6545 Synertek	5027 (9927) SMC (TI)
On-Chip Dot Timing	Yes	No	No	No	No
Synchronization Signals HSYNC/VSYNC Composite Programmable	Yes No Yes	Yes No No	Yes No Yes	Yes No Yes	Yes Yes Yes
Display Format Characters/Row Rows/Frame Scan Lines/Row	5-110 1-64 1-16	1-80 1-64 1-16	1-256 1-128 1-32	1-256 1-128 1-32	20-132* 1-64 1-16
Interlaced Mode	No	No	Yes (2)	Yes (2)	Yes
Cursor Mode Controls	Block or underline	Reverse video, blink, underline block	Reverse video, blink, block, underline	Reverse video, blink, block, underline	Block
Screen Memory Addressing Size (Max)	Linear 4K	Linear 64K	Linear 16K	Linear or Row/Column 16K	Row/Column 8K
Accessible Registers	Cursor, Top-of-Page New Row	Cursor, status, light pen	Screen format and timing registers, cursor, light pen, Top-of-Page	Screen format and timing, cursor, light pen, Top-of-Page	Cursor, scroll, Top-of-Page
On-chip Buffer	No	Two, 80-Bytes each	No	No	No
Memory Contention Logic	No	DMA	No	Transparent Memory Addressing	No
Scrolling	Yes	Yes	Yes	Yes	Yes
Visual Attributes	No	Yes	No	No	No
Light Pen Logic	No	Yes	Yes	Yes	No
Process	IIL	NMOS	NMOS	NMOS	NMOS
Power	+5 V	+5 V	+5 V	+5 V	+5 V, +12 V

* Up to 200 characters/row available in mask-programmed versions.

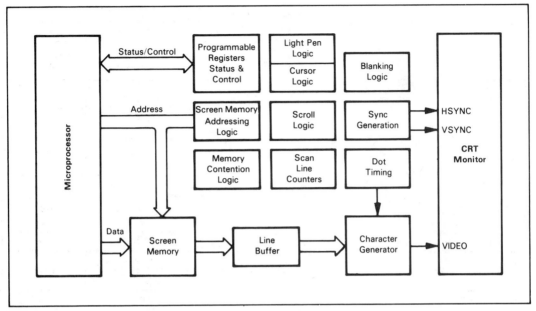

Figure 1-5. General Block Diagram of a CRT Controller

COMPARING CRT CONTROLLER DEVICES

Figure 1-5 is a generalized block diagram showing typical logic functions that must be provided to create the interface between a microprocessor and a CRT monitor. The ideal CRT controller device would incorporate all of the logic functions shown in Figure 1-5. Actual CRT controller devices, of course, do not include all of the functional blocks illustrated — it is impossible to fit that much logic on a single chip. In addition, when you implement functions on a chip you sacrifice some flexibility: the approach that the chip designer has taken when implementing the CRT controller functions will dictate, to a large extent, the approach that you must take when incorporating the device in your system. For example, inclusion of a line buffer and the character generator logic function in Figure 1-5 implies that all CRT controllers will be used to generate alphanumeric displays. This will obviously not always be the case. This also points out one of the weaknesses of Figure 1-5: the assumptions that we have made in defining logic functions that should be included in a CRT controller. Nonetheless, **we will use this illustration throughout this book to indicate the functions provided by each of the CRT controllers we will describe. While far from perfect, it does provide a starting point for comparing the capabilities of various CRT controller devices.**

The DP8350 CRT Controllers

The DP8350 CRT controller series is one of the more recently introduced set of CRT controller devices and provides some functions not available on any of the other devices described in this book. Nonetheless, because its operation is quite straightforward, we have chosen to describe the 8350 first. One reason for its relative simplicity of operation is that some of the functions which are user-programmable in other CRT controllers are mask-programmable in the DP8350s. Mask-programming of certain functions makes a great deal of sense because, while many functions need to be custom tailored to a particular design, they do not need to be altered once they have been established. The disadvantage of mask-programmable functions is, of course, that you must be a high-volume user of a particular programmed version of the DP8350 in order to justify the cost involved. If you need only a few devices and one of the standard preprogrammed versions cannot be used, you should not choose the 8350.

At this writing, the DP8350 series consists of three standard ROM versions. These are:

DP8350	80 characters/row, 24 rows, 7 × 10 field
DP8352	32 characters/row, 16 rows, 9 × 12 field
DP8353	80 characters/row, 25 rows, 9 × 12 field

However, an additional 15 ROM versions have been generated, some of which may be assigned standard part numbers in the future. If a low volume user cannot use one of the three standard versions, any of these non-standard versions may be used without having to pay for ROM mask development.

The largest functional difference between the DP8350s and the other CRT controllers we will describe is the inclusion of on-chip dot timing logic. The dot timing frequency is the highest that will be required in the CRT system and typically cannot be provided by an MOS device. The DP8350, however, is constructed using bipolar integrated-injected logic (I^2L) technology which can provide the high speed timing.

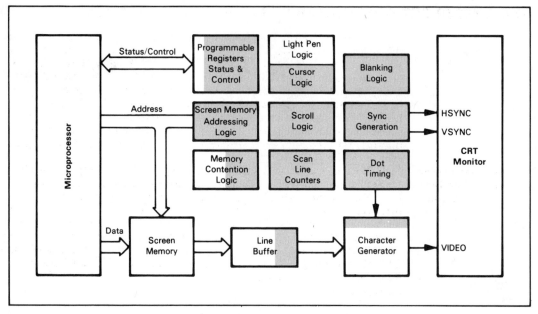

Figure 2-1. DP8350 CRT Controller Functions

The only manufacturer of the DP8350 series is:

NATIONAL SEMICONDUCTOR CORPORATION
2900 Semiconductor Drive
Santa Clara, CA 95051

Figure 2-1 illustrates those portions of the idealized CRT controller which we developed in Chapter 1 that are provided by the DP8350. Both the SYNC generation and dot timing logic are provided by the DP8350. Standard cursor and scroll logic are provided on-chip along with the screen memory addressing and scan line counter logic. The memory contention logic provided by the DP8350 is quite primitive and we have therefore shown this logic function only partially shaded. Similarly, the programmable registers provided by the 8350 are few in number, since many functions are mask-programmable. We have therefore shown this logic area as only partially present on the DP8350.

THE DP8350 CRT CONTROLLER SERIES PINS AND SIGNALS

Figure 2-2 shows the pin assignments and signals for the DP8350. At this point we will provide a brief description of each signal, since this will serve as a good introduction to, and overview of, the capabilities of this CRT controller. Our descriptions of the signals will be brief since we will discuss their uses and interrelationship in more detail later in this chapter.

The signals may be divided into three categories: signals used to interface the CRT controller to the microprocessor and system busses (we include standard power and timing input signals in this group), signals used to interface the screen memory logic and character generator logic, and signals sent to the CRT monitor.

Microprocessor Interface Signals

RSA and RSB are register select inputs that specify which of the DP8350's internal registers is to receive data from the microprocessor.

$\overline{RLD}$ is the register load signal used to strobe data into the DP8350 internal registers. The DP8350 registers that are accessible to the microprocessor are all write-only registers. In addition, there is no chip select input to the DP8350. Thus the $\overline{RLD}$ signal performs the functions of selecting the DP8350 device for a register load and actually strobing the data into the DP8350. Accordingly, the system logic used to generate $\overline{RLD}$ will have to combine both decoded address signals and the write signal from the microprocessor.

A0-A11 are dual purpose, bidirectional lines. They are used primarily as screen memory address output lines but they also serve as data inputs during register load operations.

RAE is the RAM Address Enable input. In order to use the A0-A11 address lines as data input lines, the RAE signal must be set low to place the address outputs in the high-impedance mode. It is important to note that this input does not disable any of the DP8350's internal counting logic functions; it simply disables the outputs of the screen memory address lines. Thus it is up to external logic to determine whether the DP8350 will be requiring access to the address bus before the RAE input is used to disable the address outputs. We will discuss this in more detail later in this chapter.

$\overline{SYSCLR}$ is the System Clear or reset input. When you set this signal low, it clears the Cursor and Top of Page registers within the DP8350 to zero and holds the timing chain at that point where vertical and horizontal blanking begins.

50/60 Hz. If this input is high it specifies that the CRT system refresh rate is to be 60 Hz, and if low specifies a refresh rate of 50 Hz. An interesting feature of the DP8350 is the fact that you can specify other refresh rates besides 50 and 60 Hz. The refresh rate is a mask-programmable option that you specify when you order the device. You can always specify two different frequencies for a given device. Thus, for example, you could specify a refresh rate of 37.5 Hz and 45 Hz instead of 50 Hz and 60 Hz. As part of the mask-programming specification, you assign an F_1 frequency and an F_0 frequency. A logic 1 input on the 50/60 Hz signal always selects the F_1 refresh rate, and a logic 0 selects the F_0 refresh rate.

X1 and X2 are the input connections for an external, parallel resonant crystal which will determine the operating frequency for the DP8350. The crystal frequency is the dot clock rate that will be used. You can also use a system clock instead of the crystal. In this case, the dot rate clock frequency could be applied to pin 22 (X1) from a Schottky TTL series device and pin 21 (X2) should be left opened.

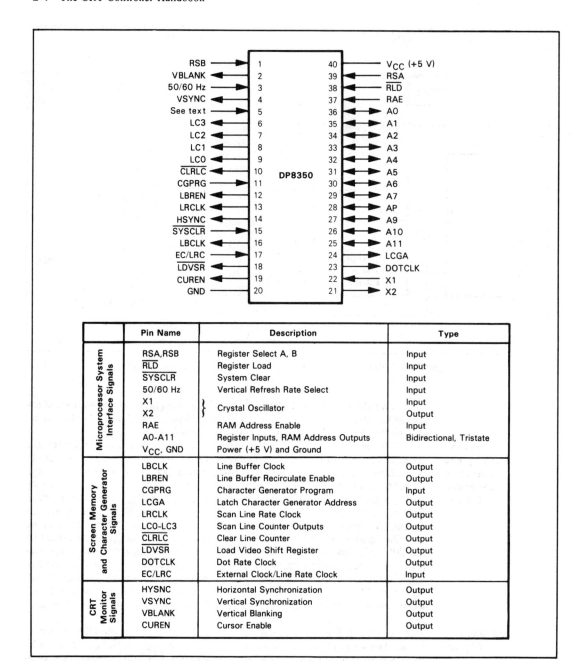

Figure 2-2. DP8350 CRT Controller Pins and Signals

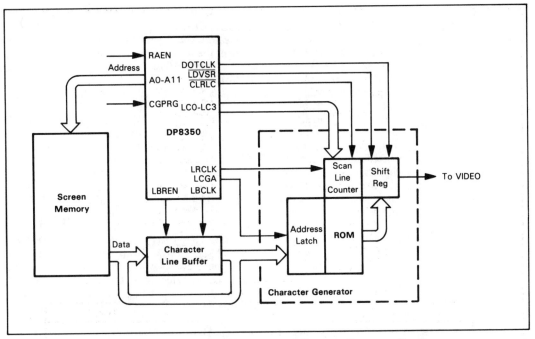

Figure 2-3. DP8350 Screen Memory and Character Generator Signals

The DOTCLK Dot Rate Clock is a buffered output at the dot rate clock frequency used for system synchronization. The positive edge of this signal should be used to clock the dot shift register.

Screen Memory and Character Generator Signals

The next group of signals we shall describe are used to interface the DP8350 to screen memory and character generator logic. A subset of signals is included in this group and provides timing for a line buffer. Since the DP8350 generates the high frequency dot clock, all of these lower frequency timing signals which are derived from that clock are also generated on-chip. That is the reason for the availability of such a large number of timing signals for the character generator and line buffer logic. No other CRT controller we describe approaches the completeness of the set of timing signals provided by the DP8350. However, not all of the signals will be required in many applications since these signals imply a very specific system organization. The system organization implied by this set of signals is nearly identical to that of our idealized CRT controller. That is, an 80-character line buffer is situated between screen memory and the character generator logic as illustrated in Figure 2-3.

Screen Memory Signals

In Figure 2-3, we have shown the signals provided by the DP8350 series for interfacing to screen memory, a line buffer, and a character generator. **The interface to screen memory simply consists of the 12 address outputs (A0-A11) and the related RAM Address Enable (RAE) signal which we have already discussed.** The 12 screen memory address outputs allow you to have up to 4096 bytes of screen memory.

Line Buffer Signals

There are three signals associated with operation of a line buffer: LBCLK, LBREN, and CGPRG. LBCLK is a Line Buffer Clock signal that is generated at the character rate and which can be used to shift the contents of the line buffer in order to present the next character address to the character generator. LBREN is the Line Buffer Recirculate Enable signal and is used to select the source of input to the character line buffer. In a typical line buffer, the recirculate enable input, when high, specifies that the character being shifted out of the line buffer is also to be used as the input to the line buffer in order to simply recirculate the contents. When the recirculate input is low, it specifies that an alternate data source (in our application, screen memory) is to be used as the input to the line buffer. Thus the line buffer is shifted and its contents recirculated until all of the scan lines that comprise a character row have been displayed; the LBREN signal is then set low so that a new line of data can be loaded into the line buffer. The LBREN signal will go low at the beginning of one horizontal blanking interval and will remain low for one scan line until the next horizontal blanking interval.

You control the scan line during which LBREN is to be low by using the Character Generator Program (CGPRG) input to the DP8350. If CGPRG is low, the LBREN signal will go low during the last scan line of a character row. If CGPRG is high, then LBREN will go low during the first scan line of a character row. This allows you to select when the line buffer should be loaded with a new line, based on whether the particular character generator you are using provides blank video during the last scan line of a character row or the first scan line.

Character Generator Signals

The remainder of the signals shown in Figure 2-3 are associated with the character generator function.

LCGA is the Latch Character Generator Address signal which is used to load a data word from the line buffer, or from screen memory if no line buffer was used, into the character generator address latch to select the character for display. The LCGA signal is generated at the character rate frequency.

The Line Rate Clock (LRCLK) signal and the four line count output signals (LC0-LC3) are all associated with the scan line count function. The LRCLK signal is used as an input to character generators which have their own internal scan line counters to increment that internal counter as each new scan line is begun. The LC0-LC3 signal is applied to a character generator that does not have an internal scan line counter to select the proper scan line address for each character. Even if you are using a character generator with an internal scan line counter, the LC0-LC3 signals may still be of use in a system. For example, you can decode these outputs to determine the current scan line of a character row. This information might be used to grant the microprocessor access to the screen memory during non-display scan lines of a character row.

The Clear Line Counter ($\overline{\text{CLRLC}}$) signal is generated after the last scan line of any character row to reset a scan line counter in preparation for the first scan line of a new character row. Thus if a character row consists of nine scan lines, the $\overline{\text{CLRLC}}$ signal will go low after the ninth scan line has been completed (LC3-LC0 = 1000_2), resetting a character generator scan line counter to 0000_2. The DP8350 will also reset its internal scan line counters at this point (LC3-LC0 = 0000_2).

The Load Video Shift Register ($\overline{\text{LDVSR}}$) signal is generated at the character rate and used to load a parallel dot pattern for a particular character into the parallel-to-serial converter shift register. The DOTCLK signal from the DP8350 is then used to clock the dot pattern out serially to create the VIDEO signal for the CRT monitor.

CRT Monitor Signals

The final group of DP8350 signals are those most directly related to the CRT monitor. There are four signals in this group: HSYNC, VSYNC, VBLANK, and CUREN.

The Horizontal Synchronization (HSYNC) and Vertical Synchronization (VSYNC) signals are the standard CRT monitor signals which we described in Chapter 1. The precise position and width of these signals and their active logic states are mask-programmable. We will describe the programming options when we discuss the programming specifications in detail later in this chapter.

The Vertical Blanking (VBLANK) signal becomes active at the start of vertical blanking — that is, upon completion of the video in the last horizontal scan line — and remains active until the beginning of the video in the first displayed scan line of the next frame. The precise scan line where the signal becomes inactive is mask-programmable, as is its polarity. The VBLANK signal may have several uses in a CRT system since it indicates a relatively long period of time when the CRT controller will not require access to the system busses.

The Cursor Enable (CUREN) signal will be output high by the DP8350 during the character time that you have specified in the Cursor register. The CUREN signal will be output either on all scan lines of a character row or on a single line; you specify your choice as part of the mask-programming procedure. Typically, the CUREN signal is logically ORed with the output of the video shift register to produce the appropriate pattern for the cursor at the proper location on the screen.

There are two pins of the DP8350 which we have not yet discussed and whose use and purpose are rather murky. Pin 5 is shown in some of the manufacturer's literature as a pin which is not to be connected (NC) and pin 17 is given the name External Character/Line Rate Clock (EC/LRC) but is described in manufacturer's literature as a test input. Pin 5 actually performs a very specific function: if it is connected to a logic "1," then it has no effect whatsoever, but if it is connected to a low or logic "0," the number of character rows you have specified during mask-programming is cut in half. For example, if you have specified that the display is to consist of 24 character rows, then only 12 character rows will be displayed if you apply a low to pin 5. The 12 character rows will be equally spaced on the CRT screen and a full row of blanks will be interspersed between each displayed row. In addition, the screen memory address outputs will be repeated while this blank row is being displayed.

THE DP8350 PROGRAMMABLE REGISTERS

The DP8350 provides three user-accessible address registers: the Top of Page register, the Row Start register, and the Cursor register. All three are 12-bit registers and are accessed via the bidirectional address lines (A0-A11). Register selection and loading is controlled by the RSA, RSB, and $\overline{RLD}$ signals according to the following table:

RSA	RSB	$\overline{RLD}$	Register Accessed
L	L	L	None
L	H	L	Top of Page
H	L	L	Row Start*
H	H	L	Cursor
X	X	H	None

X = don't care
* During vertical blanking, a load to this register also loads Top of Page

Top of Page Register

The Top of Page register contains the 12-bit screen memory address of the first word to be displayed on the screen. For example, if the Top of Page register contains $0F0_{16}$, then the data contained in screen memory location $0F0_{16}$ will be displayed in the first character position of the first character row on the screen. This can be illustrated as follows:

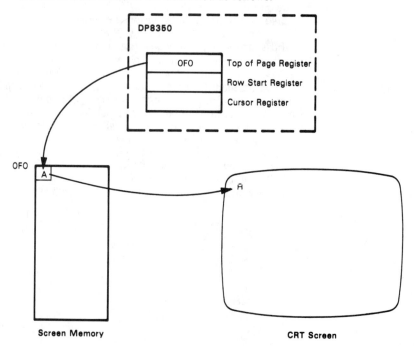

DP8350

OFO	Top of Page Register
	Row Start Register
	Cursor Register

OFO

A

Screen Memory   CRT Screen

The Top of Page register is loaded with all 0's after system clear, and its contents will not change until or unless you load a new value into this register. The most common use of the Top of Page register will be to implement scrolling; by loading the Top of Page register with a new value, you effectively move the data that is displayed on the screen. For example, if our display consists of 80-character lines, then we could scroll the screen contents up one line by adding 80 (50_{16}) to the current value held in the Top of Page register. This can be illustrated as follows:

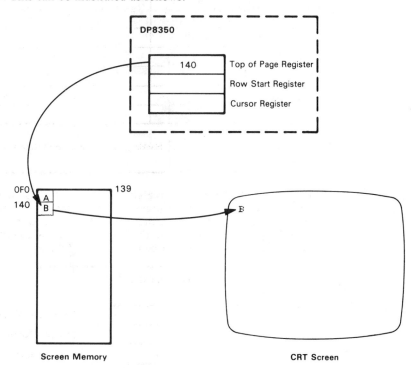

Row Start Register

The Row Start register contains the screen memory address of the first character that is to be displayed on a given character row. At the beginning of every video scan line, the DP8350's internal screen memory address counter is loaded with the contents of the Row Start register. This internal address counter is then incremented at the character rate to access each character required along the scan line. Upon completion of a scan line, the internal address counter is once again loaded with the contents of the Row Start register in preparation for displaying the next scan line of that character row. When the first character row on the screen is being displayed, the Row Start register contents will be the same as the Top of Page register as shown in the following illustration:

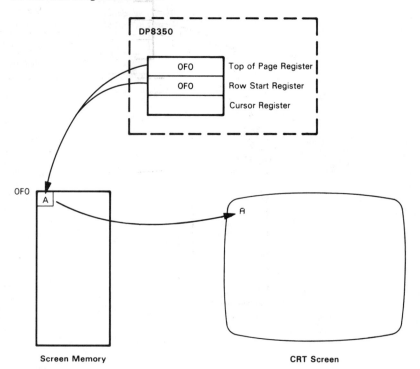

After all of the scan lines that comprise the first character row have been completed, the contents of the Row Start register are incremented to point to the screen memory location containing the first character of the next character row. For example, if our display consists of 80-character rows, then the Row Start register is loaded with a value of 140_{16} upon completion of the first character row. The DP8350's internal address counter is then loaded with this value to access the first character of the second character row:

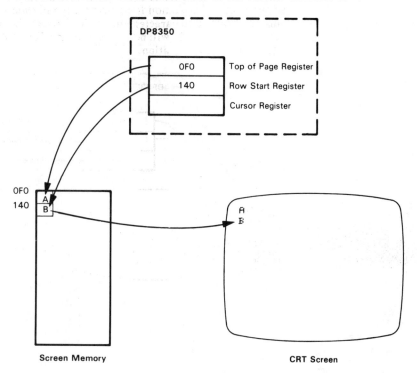

Screen Memory   CRT Screen

If the Row Start register is not loaded externally, the screen memory addresses output by the DP8350 will be sequential on a row-by-row basis beginning with the address specified by the Top of Page register and continuing through the last character line on the screen. You can, however, load the Row Start register with a new value at any time. For example, when the second character row has been displayed, you could load the Row Start register with a value of 230_{16}. Thus the first character displayed on the third row of the screen would be taken from screen memory location 230_{16} rather than 190_{16}. This can be illustrated as follows:

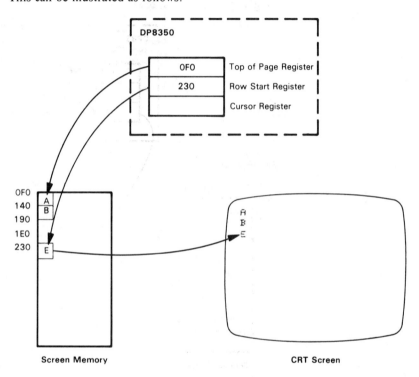

This ability to display rows of data that are not arranged sequentially in screen memory can be quite useful for text editing applications. For example, if you wish to exchange two complete character rows of data on the screen, it is not necessary to actually move any data in memory. Instead you can simply exchange the order in which the row start addresses are loaded into the Row Start register. This technique would, of course, require that you maintain an external table of Row Start addresses and that you load the desired address into the Row Start register at the beginning of each character row.

You can load the Row Start register at any time, and that new row starting address will take effect at the beginning of the next scan line. If you are manipulating the Row Start register to accomplish non-sequential row addressing, you should load the Row Start register with its next value after the start of video time of the last scan line of the current character row. If you load the Row Start register during vertical blanking, the same value will automatically be loaded into the Top of Page register since, at the beginning of the display, both the Row Start register and Top of Page register must contain the same value.

Cursor
Register

The Cursor register holds the address of the position where the cursor is to be displayed. You do not directly specify the screen location where the cursor is to appear, nor do you store a pattern representing the cursor in screen memory. Instead you load a screen memory address into the Cursor register and, when the contents of that memory address location are being displayed, the Cursor Enable (CUREN) signal will be generated to cause a cursor symbol to appear on the screen. For example, if you load the Cursor register with an address of 141_{16}, then when the contents of screen memory location 141_{16} are being displayed, the cursor will also appear on the screen. This can be illustrated as follows:

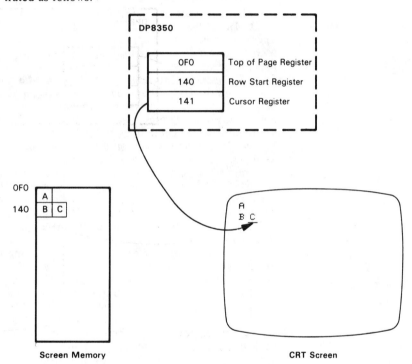

In this figure we have shown the cursor symbol as occupying a single scan line beneath the character displayed at that position. The DP8350 can also display a cursor which occupies all of the scan lines at a given character position. If this second option is implemented, the cursor symbol obliterates any character which was being displayed at that position.

The Cursor register will contain 000_{16} after a system clear. Its contents are changed only when you load a new value into the register.

THE DP8350 CRT CONTROLLER-MICROPROCESSOR INTERFACE

The interface between the DP8350 and a microprocessor is extremely simple in terms of signals that must be exchanged. There are only four control inputs to the DP8350: RSA, RSD, $\overline{RLD}$, and RAE. RSA and RSD simply select one of the DP8350's three programmable registers, and the $\overline{RLD}$ signal loads data that is applied via the A0-A11 inputs into the selected register. The RAM Address Enable (RAE) signal must be driven low in order to place the address outputs in the high impedance mode.

The DP8350 supplies no internal status register which can be read by the microprocessor to determine what the DP8350 is up to at any given instant. The DP8350 also supplies no signals specifically for status purposes. There are, however, a number of signals output by the DP8350 which can be used by a microprocessor to determine the status and progress of DP8350 operations.

The primary information requirement of a microprocessor is to determine when the DP8350 will be using the sytem busses. This will, of course, be greatly dependent on system configuration; if a line buffer is not used to hold a line of data for presentation to the character generator, then the DP8350 will require almost continuous access to the system busses. Even in this case, however, there are times when the DP8350 will not be using the busses. For example, if a character is seven scan lines high, the total character row might be comprised of nine or ten scan lines in order to provide spacing between character rows. During these "spacing" scan lines, no data will be displayed and therefore the CRT controller does not require access to the screen memory via the system busses. Since the DP8350 outputs four scan line count signals (LC0-LC3), you can simply decode these outputs to generate a bus available signal during non-display scan lines.

Similarly, since no data is displayed during vertical retrace, you can use the VBLANK signal as a bus available indication.

If a line buffer approach is used with the DP8350, the bus access requirements of the CRT controller are greatly reduced. Screen memory will only have to be accessed when the line buffer is being loaded with a fresh row of data. Thus if a character row consists of ten scan lines, the CRT controller would only require access to the screen memory during one of those scan lines while the line buffer is being reloaded. In this case, the CRT controller requires access to the system busses for less than 10% of the time.

THE DP8350 CRT CONTROLLER-SCREEN MEMORY INTERFACE

In order to understand and appreciate the interface between the DP8350 and screen memory, we must discuss it in the context of system configuration. Since the DP8350 generates such a complete set of timing signals, not all of them will be relevant in a particular system configuration. Let us begin with a simple system configuration where data from screen memory is presented directly to character generator logic. This configuration can be illustrated as follows:

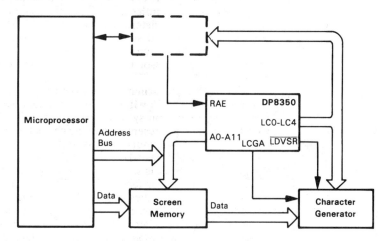

In this configuration, the DP8350 will require almost continuous access to screen memory. At the beginning of each scan line that comprises a character row, the address contained in the Row Start register will be applied to screen memory and the data from that location will then be presented to the character generator logic. The return memory addresses will be incremented at the character rate to access all of the characters that comprise that character row. This sequence can be illustrated as follows:

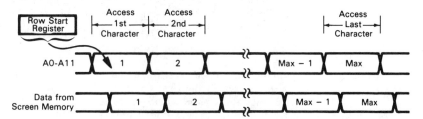

No other DP8350 timing signals are required to access screen memory and present the required data to the character generator. The RAM Address Enable (RAE) and scan line count signals (LC0-LC3) can be used by bus contention logic to determine when the microprocessor can access screen memory and use the system busses.

Screen Memory Access Lead Time

There is one subtle problem with the timing we have just illustrated: it implies that data read from screen memory is displayed immediately. This is not the case. To understand the reason for this, we must separate out the various functions that comprise the character generator logic function. The following illustration shows the three primary elements of the character generator function:

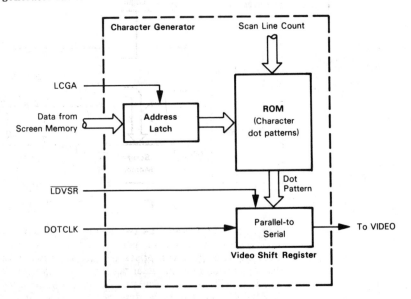

Data from screen memory serve as the symbol or character address inputs to the character generator. This address is then used to access the ROM which holds the dot pattern for that symbol. The dot pattern is read out of ROM and loaded into the parallel-to-serial shift register. The dot pattern is then shifted out serially to create the VIDEO signal.

In this sequence, two different memory devices (screen memory and the character generator ROM) must be accessed and the output from each memory device latched (into the character generator latch and video shift register respectively). Consequently, all of the access times, setup and hold times, and various settling and delay times are cumulative. Thus you must begin to access the first character for display on a scan line some time in advance of the point where you must actually begin presenting VIDEO to the CRT monitor. The DP8350 has taken these factors into consideration; it generates the first screen memory address approximately three character times ahead of the point where the first dot must be sent to the CRT monitor. For detailed information on timing, refer to the specifications in the data sheets provided at the end of this chapter.

If we add a character line buffer between screen memory and character generator logic, we can greatly reduce demands placed on system busses by the CRT logic. The DP8350 provides two timing signals (LBCLK and LBREN) which simplify implementation of a line buffer. The system configuration of a line buffer can be illustrated as follows:

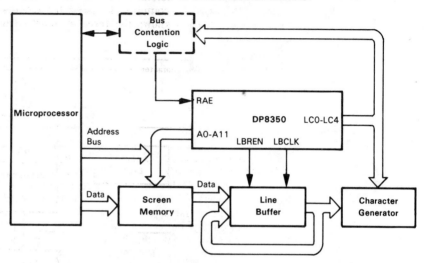

The line buffer has two modes of operation: during those scan lines which comprise the display portion of a character row, it continuously recirculates the data which comprises the character row. Prior to the beginning of the display portion of a character row, the line buffer must be loaded with the data which it will then recirculate. When the Line Buffer Recirculate Enable (LBREN) signal is high, data will be recirculated. A low level on LBREN indicates the time during which the line buffer is loaded with the next row of characters. The DP8350 sets LBREN low at the start of the horizontal blanking interval which precedes the non-display scan line where you want to load the line buffer. If the Character Generator Program input (CGPRG) is low, this will be during the last line of a character row, and if CGPRG is high it will be during the first line of a character row. The LBREN signal will remain low until the start of the next scan line.

The timing for the line buffer loading operation can be illustrated as follows:

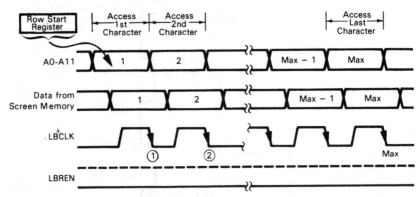

At the beginning of the non-display scan line where the line buffer is to be loaded, the DP8350 outputs the screen memory address contained in the Row Start register. The contents of this screen memory location (the first character of the character row) are read from screen memory and presented to the input of the line buffer. The LBCLK pulse generated by the DP8350 loads this first character into the line buffer and shifts the contents of the buffer one place to the right. The DP8350 increments the screen memory address to access the next character, and then generates an LBCLK pulse to load that character into the line buffer. This will be repeated, at the character rate, until all the characters comprising the complete character row have been read from screen memory and loaded into the line buffer. The LBCLK signal is not active during horizontal retrace and the number of LBCLK pulses generated is equal to the number of characters per row that you have specified.

After the line buffer has been loaded with a line of data, the LBREN signal will go high. The DP8350 then outputs an LBCLK pulse prior to the beginning of the next scan line where data is to be displayed. **The relationship of the line buffer timing to character generator logic during a scan line is illustrated in Figure 2-4.**

We have included the screen memory address outputs and the data access from screen memory in this timing diagram for purposes of establishing reference timing only. In actuality, the address outputs would be disabled using the RAE signal during this time, since the line buffer is providing the data required by the character generator.

You will notice in this figure that the first LCGA signal (which latches the output from a line buffer into the character generator address latch) occurs slightly before the active edge of the Line Buffer Clock (LBCLK) and the first character of data is shown being output from the line buffer at this point. This might be confusing at first, but recall that when we loaded the line buffer, it was shifted a number of times equal to the number of characters on a line. When we have finished loading the buffer, the first character of a line is present at the output at that point. This is the stage at which we begin a new scan line, and therefore the first character is already available from the line buffer.

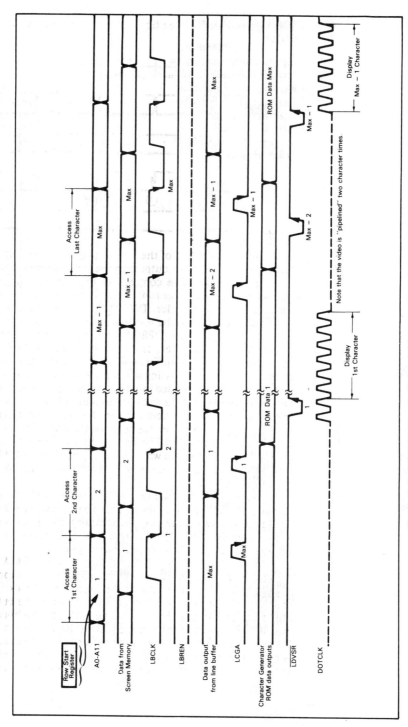

Figure 2-4. DP8350 Line Buffer and Character Generator Timing

Character Generator Logic Signals

The DP8350 provides all of the signals you will require for the interface to character generator logic. During our discussion of screen memory/line buffer timing, we described two of the character generator interface signals: Latch Character Generator Address (LCGA) and Load Video Shift Register ($\overline{\text{LDVSR}}$). In addition, the DP8350 provides six signals associated with the scan line input to character generator logic. The signals are Line Rate Clock (LRCLK), Clear Line Counter ($\overline{\text{CLRLC}}$), and four line counter outputs (LC0-LC3). The timing relationships between these signals can be illustrated as follows:

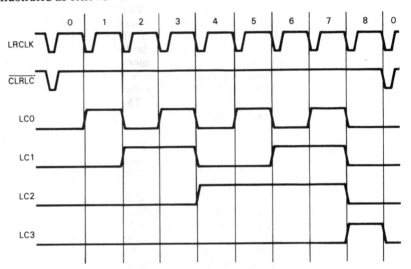

The LRCLK signal makes a positive transition near the beginning of each scan line and a negative transition at the end of the display portion of each scan line. The line counter outputs (LC0-LC3) are incremented on the negative transitions of the LRCLK signal. The line counter outputs give the binary representation of the current scan line being traced ($0\text{-}F_{16}$). The $\overline{\text{CLRLC}}$ signal occurs in synchronization with the LRCLK signal during horizontal blanking at the end of the last scan line of any character row. When the $\overline{\text{CLRLC}}$ signal goes low, the line counter outputs will all go low to represent scan line zero, the first scan line of the next character row.

Some character generator devices include a scan line counter; for these devices, you only need to use the LRCLK and $\overline{\text{CLRLC}}$ signals. As we have mentioned previously, however, the line counter outputs (LC0-LC3) may still be useful for other purposes within your system. If the character generator logic you are using does not include scan line counters, you will need the LC0-LC3 signals as inputs to the character generator logic.

CRT MONITOR INTERFACE SIGNALS

The DP8350 provides three signals (HSYNC, VSYNC, and CUREN) that are directly related to the CRT monitor interface, and two others (LDVSR and LCGA) that will be quite useful in implementing the interface.

The Horizontal Synchronization (HSYNC) and Vertical Synchronization (VSYNC) signals are the standard signals compatible with three-signal CRT monitors. The exact time at which these pulses are generated and the width of both pulses are mask-programmable. The active logic state (negative or positive pulses) of both signals is also a mask programming specification.

The HSYNC and VSYNC signals can, of course, be combined with VIDEO using external components to produce a composite video signal for the CRT monitors that require this type of input.

The Cursor Enable (CUREN) signal is generated by the DP8350 whenever the screen memory address is equal to the address contained in the Cursor register. Since there is no symbol for the cursor stored in memory, the display of the cursor on the screen must be achieved directly by bypassing character generator logic. The logic to generate a cursor symbol can be illustrated as follows:

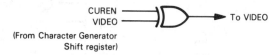

We could have used a simple OR gate so that VIDEO would be high whenever a dot was shifted out of the character generator shift register or whenever CUREN was high. That arrangement would be fine if we specified that the cursor be displayed on only one scan line and either above or below the scan lines where the characters are formed. The effect, in that case, would be the same with either an OR gate or an exclusive-OR gate. However, if we have specified that CUREN is to be high on all scan lines within a character field, the results would be different. If a standard OR gate were used, in this case, and a character were being displayed in the field where the cursor is to appear, that character would simply be overwritten by the cursor symbol since all dots within the character field would be on. With the exclusive-OR gate, however, if a character is present in a field where the block cursor symbol is to be displayed, that character will appear in reverse video, since the co-incidence of a character dot and the cursor dot will cause VIDEO to be low.

For a presentable display, the VIDEO signal to the CRT monitor must be turned off or low during horizontal and vertical retrace. The DP8350 does provide a vertical blanking (VBLANK) signal that could be used for this function during vertical retrace, but no equivalent signal is directly available during horizontal retrace. However, the Load Video Shift Register (LDVSR) signal can be used to implement this function since it is only active during the display portion of each scan line; it remains high during horizontal and vertical retrace intervals. You will recall that the LDVSR signal is a negative-going clock pulse which is used to transfer a parallel dot pattern from the character generator ROM into the parallel-to-serial shift register. Thus we would not want to use this signal directly to perform the blanking function because of the transition it makes during the display portion of the scan line. However, we can use the timing relationship that exists between

$\overline{\text{LDVSR}}$ **and the LCGA signal** to our advantage. The timing relationship between these two signals can be illustrated **as follows:**

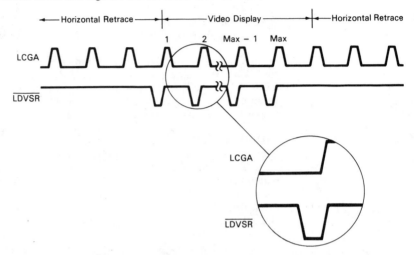

The LCGA signal is active at all times and its leading edge (negative-to-positive transition) occurs at the same time as the trailing edge (negative-to-positive transition) of $\overline{\text{LDVSR}}$. **Given this relationship, the following circuit could be used to produce the video blanking signal for both horizontal and vertical retrace:**

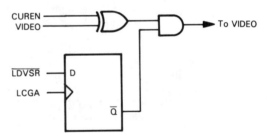

Since both $\overline{\text{LDVSR}}$ and LCGA will be going high at approximately the same time, you must use a flip-flop whose hold time requirements are near zero.

MASK-PROGRAMMING OPTIONS

Internally, the DP8350 is controlled by a ROM which determines many of the operating characteristics of the device. You can specify your own mask-programmed version of the DP8350 and thus obtain the functional characteristics needed for your particular application. Here are the options that you can specify:

- **Character size** up to 16 dots in width and 16 scan lines in height

- **Characters per row** ranging from 5 to 110

- **Character rows per frame** ranging from 1 to 64

- **Dot clock frequency** up to 25 MHz

- **VSYNC frequency** (frame refresh rate): two different frequencies can be programmed

- **HSYNC and VSYNC pulse position, duration, and polarity**

- **Cursor type** (block or single line)

Timing Chain

Many of these options are interrelated and are based upon the timing chain that you specify. Your starting point in specifying the programmable options will depend on your application and such factors as whether the most important criteria are displaying a large number of characters, displaying characters with great resolution, using widely available low-cost CRT monitors, and so on. Let us begin by seeing what some of the limits are on the timing chain specification.

The timing chain illustration that follows is the generalized one we developed in Chapter 1 with maximum allowable values for the DP8350 inserted:

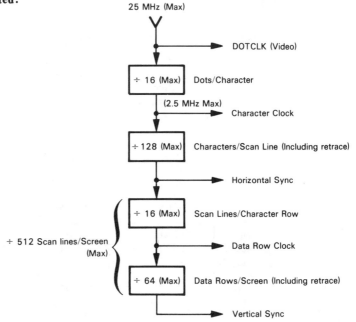

The values shown in this illustration should be viewed as separate entities, each representing the maximum possible value that could be included in a timing chain developed around that box. The interrelationship of various elements of the timing chain also imposes certain limitations on the programming options you can specify. For example, the maximum dot clock frequency permitted is 25 MHz and the maximum character rate frequency is 2.5 MHz. If you are using a 25 MHz dot clock, the mimimum number of dots per character along a scan line is ten, since a lesser number would produce a character clock exceeding 2.5 MHz.

There are several programming specification limitations that are implied in the manufacturer's literature but not directly stated. For example, we stated at the outset of this discussion that you can specify from 5 to 110 characters per character row. Internally, the DP8350 uses a 7-bit counter to count character times, making the maximum number of character times per scan line 128. This upper limit of 128 also includes horizontal retrace time, since the DP8350 uses the character rate clock to time this function also. Rather than stating an upper limit of 110 characters per row, it is more meaningful to state that the number of characters per row, plus horizontal retrace time expressed in character times, cannot exceed 128.

A similar limitation exists with the maximum number of character lines per frame that you can specify. You can specify that a character row be comprised of up to 16 scan lines and you can specify as many as 64 character rows per frame. If you specify these maximum numbers for both, the total number of scan lines per frame is 1024. However, the DP8350 uses a 9-bit counter to count lines per frame; this imposes an upper limit of 512 scan lines per frame, and the time required for vertical retrace must also be taken out of the 512 scan line times. Thus, while the maximum values of scan lines per character and character rows per frame are 16 and 64 as we stated at the outset, the total number of scan lines per frame including vertical retrace time cannot exceed 512.

The DP8350 Series Option Program Table

Table 2-1 is a reproduction of the table you use to specify how you want the DP8350 ROM mask-programmed to obtain the operating characteristics you require. Most of the entries in Table 2-1 are self-explanatory and consist either of establishing elements of the timing chain or positioning and defining the duration of various pulses within the timing chain. We will begin our discussion with the entries at the top of the table. In practice, however, your starting point might be elsewhere, depending on the primary operating criteria for your application. For example, if it is important that you be able to use a widely available commercial CRT monitor, you will first establish dot clock, HSYNC, and VSYNC frequencies that are compatible with those CRT monitors.

The first four entries in Table 2-1 define the size of characters that will be displayed. Entries 1 and 2 specify the size of the actual character itself, while entires 3 and 4 define the size of the field within which the character will be displayed. Entries 1 and 2 are therefore actually irrelevant and do nothing to determine the operating characteristics of a DP8350; dot timing, character timing, scan line timing, and so on will all be derived from the specified size of the character field. The character generator logic which you use in conjunction with DP8350 uses these timing signals to produce the desired character size within the field.

Table 2-1. DP8350 Series Option Program Table

Item No.	Parameter		Value	
1	Character (Font Size)	Dots per Character		
2		Scan Lines per Character		
3	Character Field (Block Size)	Dots per Character		
4		Scan Lines per Character		
5	Number of Video Characters per Row			
6	Number of Video Character Rows per Frame			
7	Number of Video Scan Lines (Item 4 × Item 6)			
8	Frame Refresh Rate (Hz) (two frequencies allowed)			
9	Delay after/before Vertical Blank start to start of Vertical sync (+/− Number of Scan Lines)		f1 =	f0 =
10	Vertical Sync Width (Number of Scan Lines)			
11	Delay after Vertical Blank start to start of Video (Number of Scan Lines)			
12	Total Scan Lines per Frame (Item 7 + item 11 = 13 ÷ Item 8)			
13	Horizontal Scan Frequency (Line Rate) (kHz) Item 8 × Item 12			
14	Number of Character Times per Scan Line			
15	Character Clock Rate (MHz) Item 13 × Item 14			
16	Character Time (ns) (1 ÷ Item 15)			
17	Delay after/before Horizontal Blank start to Horizontal Sync start (+/− Character Times)			
18	Horizontal Sync Width (Character Times)			
19	Dot Frequency (MHz) (Item 3 × Item 15)			
20	Dot Time (ns) (1 ÷ Item 19)			
21	Vertical Blanking Stop before start of Video (Number of Scan Lines) (Range = Item 4 − 1 line to 0 lines)			
22	Cursor Enable on all Scan Lines of a Row? (Yes or No) If not, which Line?			
23	Does the Horizontal Sync pulse have Serrations during Vertical Sync? (Yes or No)			
24	Width of Line Buffer Clock logic "0" state within a Character Time (Number of Dot Time increments)			
25	Serration Pulse Width, if used (Character Times)			
26	Horizontal Sync Pulse Active state logic level (1 or 0)			
27	Vertical Sync Pulse Active state logic level (1 or 0)			
28	Vertical Blanking Pulse Active state logic level (1 or 0)			

Note 1: If the Cursor Enable, Item 22, is active on only one line of a character row, then Item 21 must be either "1" or "0" unless it is the same as the line selected for Cursor Enable.

Note 2: Item 24 × Item 20 should be > 250 ns.

Note 3: Item 11 must be greater than item 4 + 1.

This table is reprinted by permission of National Semiconductor, Inc.

Table 2-2. DP8350 Program Table*

Item No.	Parameter		Value	
1	Character (Font Size)	Dots per Character	5	
2		Scan Lines per Character	7	
3	Character Field (Block Size)	Dots per Character	7	
4		Scan Lines per Character	10	
5	Number of Video Characters per Row		80	
6	Number of Video Character Rows per Frame		24	
7	Number of Video Scan Lines (Item 4 × Item 6)		240	
8	Frame Refresh Rate (Hz) (two frequencies allowed)		f1 = 60	f0 = 50
9	Delay after/before Vertical Blank start to start of Vertical sync (+/− Number of Scan Lines)		4	30
10	Vertical Sync Width (Number of Scan Lines)		10	10
11	Delay after Vertical Blank start to start of Video (Number of Scan Lines)		20	72
12	Total Scan Lines per Frame (Item 7 + item 11 = 13 ÷ Item 8)		260	312
13	Horizontal Scan Frequency (Line Rate) (kHz) Item 8 × Item 12		15.6 KHz	
14	Number of Character Times per Scan Line		100	
15	Character Clock Rate (MHz) Item 13 × Item 14		1.56 MHz	
16	Character Time (ns) (1 ÷ Item 15)		641 ns	
17	Delay after/before Horizontal Blank start to Horizontal Sync start (+/− Character Times)		0	
18	Horizontal Sync Width (Character Times)		43	
19	Dot Frequency (MHz) (Item 3 × Item 15)		10.92 MHz	
20	Dot Time (ns) (1 ÷ Item 19)		91.6 ns	
21	Vertical Blanking Stop before start of Video (Number of Scan Lines) (Range = Item 4 − 1 line to 0 lines)		1	
22	Cursor Enable on all Scan Lines of a Row? (Yes or No) If not, which Line?		Yes	
23	Does the Horizontal Sync pulse have Serrations during Vertical Sync? (Yes or No)		No	
24	Width of Line Buffer Clock logic "0" state within a Character Time (Number of Dot Time increments)		4	
25	Serration Pulse Width, if used (Character Times)		N/A	
26	Horizontal Sync Pulse Active state logic level (1 or 0)		1	
27	Vertical Sync Pulse Active state logic level (1 or 0)		0	
28	Vertical Blanking Pulse Active state logic level (1 or 0)		1	

Note 4: Horizontal and Vertical sync pulses are compatible with Ball
Brothers TV-12 or TV-120 series monitors or equivalents.

* 80 characters/row × 24 character rows, 7 × 10-character cell dot matrix

Table 2-3. DP8352 Program Table*

Item No.	Parameter		Value	
1	Character (Font Size)	Dots per Character	7	
2		Scan Lines per Character	9	
3	Character Field (Block Size)	Dots per Character	9	
4		Scan Lines per Character	12	
5	Number of Video Characters per Row		32	
6	Number of Video Character Rows per Frame		16	
7	Number of Video Scan Lines (Item 4 × Item 6)		192	
8	Frame Refresh Rate (Hz) (two frequencies allowed)		f1 = 60	f0 = 50
9	Delay after/before Vertical Blank start to start of Vertical sync (+/− Number of Scan Lines)		27	53
10	Vertical Sync Width (Number of Scan Lines)		3	3
11	Delay after Vertical Blank start to start of Video (Number of Scan Lines)		68	120
12	Total Scan Lines per Frame (Item 7 + item 11 = 13 ÷ Item 8)		260	312
13	Horizontal Scan Frequency (Line Rate) (kHz) Item 8 × Item 12		15.6 kHz	
14	Number of Character Times per Scan Line		50	
15	Character Clock Rate (MHz) Item 13 × Item 14		0.78 MHz	
16	Character Time (ns) (1 ÷ Item 15)		1282 ns	
17	Delay after/before Horizontal Blank start to Horizontal Sync start (+/− Character Times)		6	
18	Horizontal Sync Width (Character Times)		4	
19	Dot Frequency (MHz) (Item 3 × Item 15)		7.02 MHz	
20	Dot Time (ns) (1 ÷ Item 19)		142.4 ns	
21	Vertical Blanking Stop before start of Video (Number of Scan Lines) (Range = Item 4 − 1 line to 0 lines)		0	
22	Cursor Enable on all Scan Lines of a Row? (Yes or No) If not, which Line?		Yes	
23	Does the Horizontal Sync pulse have Serrations during Vertical Sync? (Yes or No)		Yes	
24	Width of Line Buffer Clock logic "0" state within a Character Time (Number of Dot Time increments)		5	
25	Serration Pulse Width, if used (Character Times)		4	
26	Horizontal Sync Pulse Active state logic level (1 or 0)		0	
27	Vertical Sync Pulse Active state logic level (1 or 0)		0	
28	Vertical Blanking Pulse Active state logic level (1 or 0)		1	

Note 4: Horizontal and Vertical sync pulses are RS170 Compatible.

* 32 characters/row × 16 character rows, 9 × 12-character cell dot matrix

This table is reprinted by permission of National Semiconductor, Inc.

Table 2-4. DP8353 Program Table*

Item No.	Parameter		Value	
1	Character (Font Size)	Dots per Character	7	
2		Scan Lines per Character	9	
3	Character Field (Block Size)	Dots per Character	9	
4		Scan Lines per Character	12	
5	Number of Video Characters per Row		80	
6	Number of Video Character Rows per Frame		25	
7	Number of Video Scan Lines (Item 4 × Item 6)		300	
8	Frame Refresh Rate (Hz) (two frequencies allowed)		f1 = 60	f0 = 50
9	Delay after/before Vertical Blank start to start of Vertical sync (+/− Number of Scan Lines)		0	32
10	Vertical Sync Width (Number of Scan Lines)		3	3
11	Delay after Vertical Blank start to start of Video (Number of Scan Lines)		20	84
12	Total Scan Lines per Frame (Item 7 + item 11 = 13 ÷ Item 8)		320	384
13	Horizontal Scan Frequency (Line Rate) (kHz) Item 8 × Item 12		19.20 kHz	
14	Number of Character Times per Scan Line		102	
15	Character Clock Rate (MHz) Item 13 × Item 14		1.9584 MHz	
16	Character Time (ns) (1 ÷ Item 15)		510.6 ns	
17	Delay after/before Horizontal Blank start to Horizontal Sync start (+/− Character Times)		5	
18	Horizontal Sync Width (Character Times)		9	
19	Dot Frequency (MHz) (Item 3 × Item 15)		17.6256 MHz	
20	Dot Time (ns) (1 ÷ Item 19)		56.7 ns	
21	Vertical Blanking Stop before start of Video (Number of Scan Lines) (Range = Item 4 − 1 line to 0 lines)		1	
22	Cursor Enable on all Scan Lines of a Row? (Yes or No) If not, which Line?		Yes	
23	Does the Horizontal Sync pulse have Serrations during Vertical Sync? (Yes or No)		No	
24	Width of Line Buffer Clock logic "0" state within a Character Time (Number of Dot Time increments)		5	
25	Serration Pulse Width, if used (Character Times)		N/A	
26	Horizontal Sync Pulse Active state logic level (1 or 0)		1	
27	Vertical Sync Pulse Active state logic level (1 or 0)		1	
28	Vertical Blanking Pulse Active state logic level (1 or 0)		1	

Note 4: Horizontal and Vertical sync pulses are compatible with Motorola M3000 series monitors or equivalents.

* 80 characters/row × 25 character rows, 9 × 12-character cell dot matrix

This table is reprinted by permission of National Semiconductor, Inc.

Item #5 in the option program table specifies the number of displayed characters per row. This in turn establishes the number of LDVSR pulses per line. Item #14 is the number of character times per scan line and includes the horizontal retrace delay. Thus, item #5 plus the horizontal retrace delay stated in character times is equal to item #14, which in turn determines the character clock rate for the DP8350.

Item #7 indicates the number of displayable scan lines per frame and is the product of scan lines per character (item #4) and character rows per frame (item #6). As we discussed earlier, this value, plus the vertical retrace time expressed in scan lines, cannot exceed 512; thus, the maximum value for item #12 is 512.

Vertical retrace takes place during vertical blanking, which is automatically initiated at the end of the last displayed scan line. The duration of the non-video portion during vertical retrace is defined in terms of scan lines in item #11. The starting point for the VSYNC pulse and its duration are defined by items #9 and #10 respectively. The following illustration shows the relationships between VBLANK, VSYNC, and the video portion of each frame:

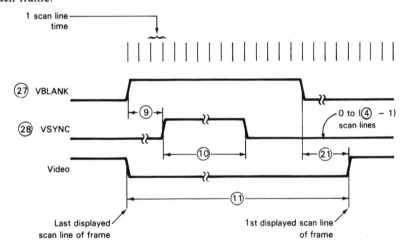

Items #27 and #28 simply specify the polarity, or active logic state, for the VBLANK and VSYNC signals.

The HSYNC frequency is specified in item #13. It is the product of vertical refresh rate (item #8) times total scan lines per frame (item #12). It can also be derived, of course, by dividing the character clock rate (item #15) by the number of character times per scan line (item #14), depending on which direction you are working along the timing chain. **The position and duration of the HSYNC pulse in relation to the horizontal blanking or non-video portion of each scan line are specified in items #17 and #18 respectively. This relationship can be illustrated as follows:**

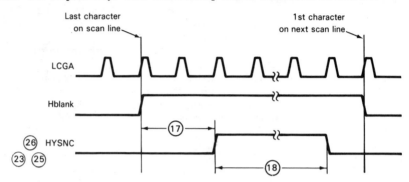

The polarity of the HSYNC pulse is specified in item #26. Items #23 and #25 define whether the HSYNC pulse is to have serrations during vertical retrace time. These serrations may be required with some monitors and, if so, the pulse widths of the serrations are specified in item #25.

The following illustration shows how the various entries in the DP8350 series option program table relate to the generalized timing chain which we developed in Chapter 1.

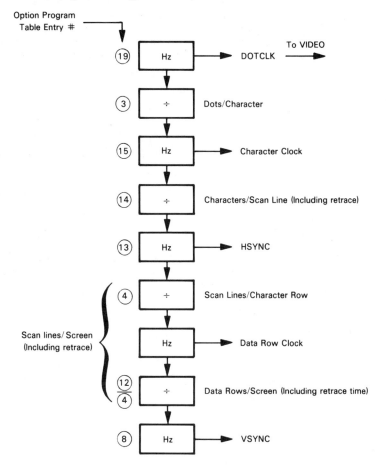

Tables 2-2, 2-3, and 2-4 are option program tables for the preprogrammed devices available.

DATA SHEETS

This section contains specific electrical and timing data for the DP8350.

DP8350

Crystal Inputs X1 and X2: The "Pierce"-type oscillator is controlled by an external crystal providing parallel resonant operation. Connection of external bias components is made to pin 22 (X1) and pin 21 (X2) as shown in Figure 6. It is important that the crystal be mounted in close proximity to the X1 and X2 pins to ensure that printed circuit trace lengths are kept to an absolute minimum. Typical specifications for the crystal are shown in Table 4 for each of the standard products, DP8350, DP8352, and DP8353. When customer mask options require higher frequencies, it may be necessary to change the crystal specifications and biasing components. If the CRTC is to be clocked by an external system dot clock, pin 22 (X1) should be driven directly by Schottky family logic while pin 21 (X2) is left open. The typical threshold for pin 22 (X1) is $V_{CC}/2$.

Table 4. Typical Crystal Specifications

Parameter	Specification		
	DP8350	DP8352	DP8353
Type	At-Cut		
Frequency	10.92 MHz	7.02 MHz	17.6256 MHz
Tolerance	0.005% at 25°C		
Stability	0.01% from 0°C to +70°C		
Resonance	Fundamental, Parallel		
Maximum Series Resistance	50Ω		
Load Capacitance	20 pF		

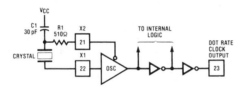

Figure 6. Dot Clock Oscillator Configuration with Typical External Bias Circuitry Shown

Custom Order Mask Programmability: The DP8350 Series CRT controller is available in three standard options designated DP8350, DP8352, and DP8353. The functional format of these devices was selected to meet the typical needs of CRT terminal designs. In order to accommodate specific customer formats, the DP8350 series CRT controller is mask programmable with a diverse range of options available. The items listed in the program table worksheet indicate the available options, while Table 5 tabulates the programming constraints.

Table 5. Mask Programming Limitations

Desig-nation	Parameter		Min. Value	Max. Value
f_{DOT}	Dot Rate Frequency		DC	30 MHz
f_{CHAR}	Character Rate Frequency		DC	2.5 MHz
—	Line Buffer Clock Logic "0" Width (Item 20 × Item 24)		200 ns	
Item 3	Dots per Character Field Width		4	16
Item 4	Scan Lines per Character Field		2	16
Item 12	Scan Lines per Frame			512
Item 14	Character Times per Row	Video	5	122
		Blanking	6	123
Item 11	Scan Lines per Vertical Blanking		(Item 4) + 2	

If the cursor enable output, Item 22, is active on only one line of a character row, then Item 21 value must be either "1" or "0" or equivalent to the line selected for the cursor enable output.

DP8350

Absolute Maximum Ratings (Note 1)

Supply Voltage, V_{CC}	7.0V
Input Voltage	5.5V
Output Voltage	5.5V
Storage Temperature Range	'65°C to ¹150°C
Lead Temperature (soldering, 10 seconds)	300°C

Operating Conditions (Note 6)

	Min.	Max.	Units
V_{CC}, Supply Voltage	4.75	5.25	V
T_A, Ambient Temperature	0	¹70	°C

Electrical Characteristics $V_{CC} = 5V \pm 5\%$, $T_A = 0°C$ to $+70°C$ (Notes 2, 3, and 5)

	Parameter	Conditions	Min.	Typ.	Max.	Units
V_{IH}	Logic "1" Input Voltage					
	All Inputs Except X1, X2 $\overline{RESET}$		2.0			V
	$\overline{RESET}$		2.6			V
V_{IL}	Logic "0" Input Voltage					
	All Inputs Except X1, X2				0.8	V
V_{HYS}	$\overline{RESET}$ Input Hysteresis			0.4		V
V_{clamp}	Input Clamp Voltage					
	All Inputs Except X1, X2	$I_{IN} = -12mA$		-0.8	-1.2	V
I_{IH}	Logic "1" Input Current					
	$A_0 - A_{11}$	Enable Input = 0V, $V_{CC} = 5.25V$, $V_{IN} = 5.25V$		10	100	µA
	All Other Inputs Except X1, X2	$V_{CC} = 5.25V$, $V_{IN} = 5.25V$		2	20	µA
I_{IL}	Logic "0" Input Current					
	$A_0 - A_{11}$	Enable Input = 0V, $V_{CC} = 5.25V$, $V_{IN} = 0.5V$		-20	-100	µA
	All Other Inputs Except X1, X2	$V_{CC} = 5.25V$, $V_{IN} = 0.5V$		-20	-100	µA
V_{OH}	Logic "1" Output Voltage	$I_{OH} = -100µA$	3.2	4.1		V
		$I_{OH} = -1mA$	2.5	3.3		V
V_{OL}	Logic "0" Output Voltage	$I_{OL} = 5mA$		0.35	0.5	V
I_{OS}	Output Short Circuit Current	$V_{CC} = 5V$, $V_{OUT} = 0V$ (Note 4)	10	40	100	mA
I_{CC}	Power Supply Current	$V_{CC} = 5.25V$		185	260	mA

Note 1: "Absolute Maximum Ratings" are those values beyond which the safety of the device cannot be guaranteed. They are not meant to imply that the device should be operated at these limits. The table of "Electrical Characteristics" provides conditions for actual device operation.

Note 2: Unless otherwise specified, min./max. limits apply across the 0°C to +70°C temperature range and the 4.75V to 5.25V power supply range. All typical values are for $T_A = 25°C$ and $V_{CC} = 5.0V$ and are intended for reference only.

Note 3: All currents into device pins are shown as positive; all currents out of device pins are shown as negative; all voltages are referenced to ground, unless otherwise specified. All values shown as max. or min. are so classified on absolute value basis.

Note 4: Only one output at a time should be shorted.

Note 5: Electrical specifications do not apply to pin 17, external char/line clock, as this pin is used for production testing only.

Note 6: Functional operation of device is not guaranteed when operated beyond specified operating condition limits.

Switching Characteristics $V_{CC} = 5.0V \pm 5\%$, $T_A = 25°C$ (Note 7)

	Parameter	Load Circuit	Notes	Min.	Typ.	Max.	Units
Symmetry	Dot Rate Clock Output High Symmetry With Crystal Control	1		$50\% - 4$	$50\% - 2$	$50\% + 1$	ns
t_{pd1}	XI Input to Dot Rate Clock Output Positive Edge	1			17	22	ns
t_{pd0}	XI Input to Dot Rate Clock Output Negative Edge	1			21	26	ns
t_{D1}	Dot Clock to Load Video Shift Register Negative Edge	1			6	10	ns
t_{D2}	Dot Clock to Load Video Shift Register Positive Edge	1			11	15	ns
t_{D3}	Dot Clock to Latch Character Generator Positive Edge	1			8	13	ns
t_{D4}	Dot Clock to Latch Character Generator Negative Edge	1			6	10	ns

DP8350

Switching Characteristics (cont'd) $V_{CC} = 5.0\,V \pm 5\%$, $T_A = 25\,°C$ (Note 7)

	Parameter	Load Circuit	Notes	Min.	Typ.	Max.	Units
$t_{D2} - t_{D3}$	Latch Character Generator Positive Edge to Load Video Shift Register Postive Edge	1		0	3		ns
t_{D5}	Dot Clock to Line Buffer Clock Negative Edge	1			23	35	ns
t_{PW1}	Line Buffer Clock Pulse Width	1	8,9	N(DT)	N(DT)+8	N(DT)+12	ns
t_{D6}	Dot Clock to Cursor Enable Output Transition	1			24	36	ns
t_{D7}	Dot Clock to Valid Address Output	1			15	25	ns
t_{D8}	Latch Character Generator to Line Rate Clock Transition	1	8		380 + DT	500 + DT	ns
t_{D9}	Latch Character Generator to Clear Line Counter Transition	1	8		480 + DT	700 + DT	ns
t_{D10}	Line Rate Clock to Line Counter Output Transition	1			60	120	ns
t_{D11}	Line Rate Clock to Line Buffer Recirculate Enable Transition	1			195	300	ns
t_{D12}	Line Rate Clock to Vertical Blanking Transition	1			160	300	ns
t_{D13}	Line Rate Clock to Vertical Sync Transition	1			220	300	ns
t_{D14}	Latch Character Generator to Horizontal Sync Transition	1			96	150	ns
t_{S1}	Register Select Set-up Before Register Load Negative Edge			0			ns
t_{H1}	Register Select Hold After Register Load Positive Edge			0			ns
t_{S2}	Valid Address Input Set-Up Before Register Load Positive Edge			250			ns
t_{H2}	Valid Address Hold Time After Register Load Positive Edge			0			ns
t_{PW2}	Register Load Required Pulse Width			150	65		ns
t_{LZ}, t_{HZ}	Delay from Enable Input to Address Output High Impedance State from Logic "0" and Logic "1"	2			15	30	ns
t_{ZL}, t_{ZH}	Delay from Enable Input to Logic "0" and Logic "1" from Address Output High Impedance State	2			17	30	ns

Note 7: Typical values are for $V_{CC} = 5.0V$ and $T_A = 25\,°C$ and are meant for reference only.

Note 8: "DT" denotes dot rate clock period time, item 20 from option format table.

Note 9: "N" denotes value of item 24 from option format table.

Switching Load Circuits

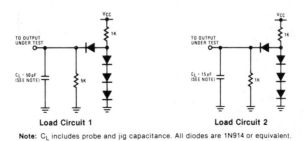

Load Circuit 1   **Load Circuit 2**

Note: C_L includes probe and jig capacitance. All diodes are 1N914 or equivalent.

DP8350

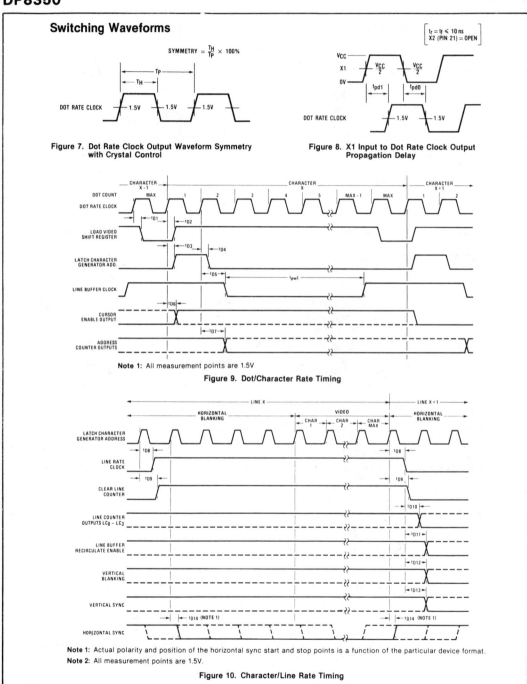

Switching Waveforms

$$\text{SYMMETRY} = \frac{T_H}{T_P} \times 100\%$$

$$\left[\begin{array}{l} t_r = t_f \leqslant 10 \text{ ns} \\ \text{X2 (PIN 21) = OPEN} \end{array}\right]$$

Figure 7. Dot Rate Clock Output Waveform Symmetry with Crystal Control

Figure 8. X1 Input to Dot Rate Clock Output Propagation Delay

Note 1: All measurement points are 1.5V

Figure 9. Dot/Character Rate Timing

Note 1: Actual polarity and position of the horizontal sync start and stop points is a function of the particular device format.

Note 2: All measurement points are 1.5V.

Figure 10. Character/Line Rate Timing

DP8350

Switching Waveforms (cont'd)

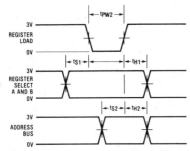

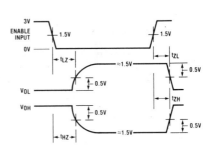

Note 1: All measurement points are 1.5V.
Note 2: $t_r = t_f \leqslant 10\,ns$.
Note 3: Address enable (pin 37) = 0V.

Figure 11. Register Select and Load Waveforms

Figure 12. Address Output Enable/Disable Waveforms

Timing Diagrams

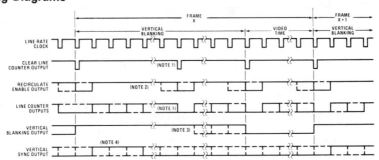

Note 1: One full row before start of video the line counter is set to zero state — this provides line counter synchronization in cases where the number of lines in vertical blanking are not even multiples of the number of lines per row.

Note 2: The position of the line buffer recirculate enable logic low level is a function of the logic level of the address mode input (see Table 3).

Note 3: The stop point of the vertical blanking output active signal is a function of device type or custom option, and will always be within one row prior to video.

Note 4: The transition start and stop points of the vertical sync output signal are a function of device type or custom option.

Figure 14. Line/Frame Rate Functional Diagram

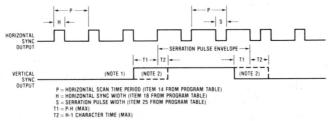

P = HORIZONTAL SCAN TIME PERIOD (ITEM 14 FROM PROGRAM TABLE)
H = HORIZONTAL SYNC WIDTH (ITEM 18 FROM PROGRAM TABLE)
S = SERRATION PULSE WIDTH (ITEM 25 FROM PROGRAM TABLE)
T1 = P-H (MAX)
T2 = H-1 CHARACTER TIME (MAX)

Note 1: The vertical sync transition point is always coincident with the beginning of horizontal blanking.

Note 2: T1 and T2 intervals represent the range of alignment offset between the vertical sync pulse and the serration pulse envelope and is a function of the horizontal sync position with respect to the beginning of horizontal blanking.

Figure 15. Serration Pulse Format

DP8350

Timing Diagrams (cont'd)

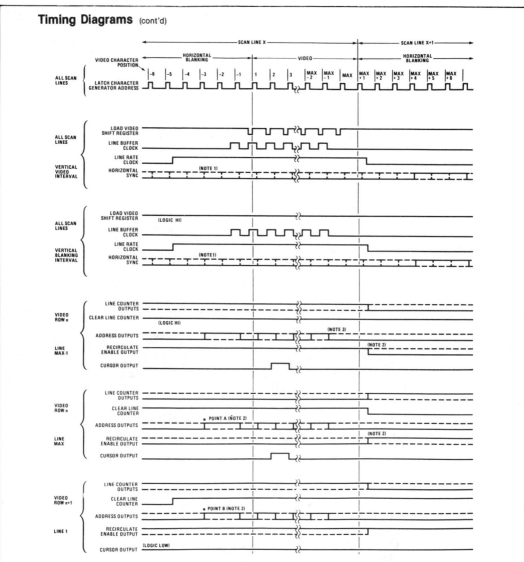

Note 1: The horizontal sync output start and stop point positions are a function of device type or custom option.

Note 2: The position of the recirculate enable output logic "0" level is dependent on the state of the address mode input. When address mode = "0", recirculate enable occurs on the max. line of a character row (solid line) and the address counter outputs roll over to the new row address at point A. When address mode = "1", recirculate enable occurs on the first line of a character row (dashed line) and the address counter outputs roll over to the new row address at point B.

Note 3: The address counter outputs clock to the address of the last character of a video row plus 1. This address is then held during the horizontal blanking interval until video minus three character times. At this point the outputs are modified to the contents of the Row Start Register (RSR).

Figure 13. Character/Line Rate Functional Diagram

3

The 8275 CRT Controller

The 8275 CRT controller represents an interesting contrast to the DP8350 device described in the preceding chapter. The designers of these two chips have taken completely different approaches to implementing the controller function. While both devices allow you to specify many options, such as character size and timing chain parameters, the 8275 options are specified under program control instead of being mask-programmed as in the DP8350.

The unique feature of the 8275 CRT controller is the inclusion of two 80-character buffers within the device. The presence of these data buffers and the microprocessor interface logic provided by the 8275 imply, and in fact demand, a very specific system configuration — one that is quite different from that which would be used with the DP8350.

Figure 3-1 illustrates those logic functions of the idealized CRT controller, which we described in Chapter 1, that are provided by the 8275. The two most notable aspects of this figure are the presence of line buffer logic and the absence of any refresh memory addressing logic. The 8275 device will often be used in conjunction with a DMA controller such as the 8257. The DMA controller generates the screen memory addresses and loads the data that is to be displayed into the 8275's row buffers.

Figure 3-1 indicates that the 8275 device provides memory contention logic, but no scrolling logic. The memory contention logic actually consists of those signals used to interface to the DMA controller; the 8275 device simply waits for external logic (such as a DMA controller) to provide it with data it has requested. The scrolling function is also performed via external logic; scrolling is easily implemented in an 8275 system but is performed transparently so far as the 8275 device itself is concerned.

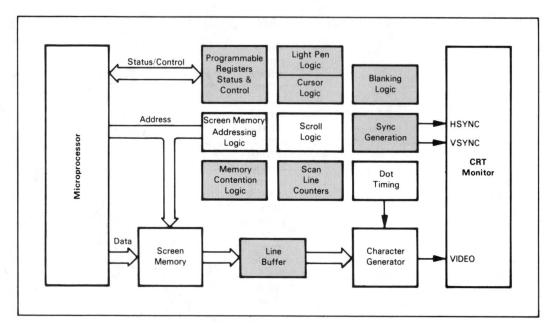

Figure 3-1. 8275 CRT Controller Function Logic

The 8275 does not provide any dot timing logic but does generate the lower frequency scan line counter signals and HSYNC and VSYNC timing signals. The cursor logic and blanking logic provided by the 8275 is quite extensive and allows you to easily implement a number of options with a minimum of external circuitry. Light pen logic is also provided by the 8275. The sole manufacturer of the 8275 device is:

INTEL CORPORATION
3065 Bowers Avenue
Santa Clara, CA 95051

THE 8275 CRT CONTROLLER PINS AND SIGNALS

Figure 3-2 shows the pin assignments and signals for the 8275. We will provide a brief description of each signal since this will serve as a good introduction to, and overview of, the capabilities of the 8275. We will discuss the uses of the signals and their interrelationships in more detail later in this chapter.

The 8275 signals may be divided into three categories: signals used to interface the controller to the microprocessor and system busses, signals used to interface the controller to character generator logic, and signals directly related to the controller-CRT monitor interface.

The microprocessor system-controller interface signals are described below.

Microprocessor Interface Signals

$\overline{CS}$ is a standard chip select input signal which would typically be generated by system address decoding logic. $\overline{CS}$ must be low in order to read status from, or write commands to, the 8275. Note that the $\overline{CS}$ signal must remain inactive when writing display data into the 8275's row buffers since this is performed under control of external (DMA) logic.

A0 is the register address input that specifies which of the 8275's internal registers is to be accessed by a read or write operation.

$\overline{RD}$ is the Read signal that controls the output of status data or parameters from the 8275 onto the data bus.

$\overline{WR}$ is the Write signal that must be low when command or parameter information is to be written into one of the 8275's internal registers. It is also active when data is written into the row buffers.

DB0-DB7 are the data bus lines used to exchange 8-bit parallel bytes of information between the 8275 and the microprocessor system. These 8 tri-state lines are bidirectional.

IRQ is an Interrupt Request output. You can program the 8275 so that an interrupt request will be generated at the end of each frame when the last display row of the screen is begun.

DRQ is the DMA Request signal used to request transfer of data from memory to the 8275 row buffers.

The $\overline{DACK}$ input is the DMA Acknowledge signal from a DMA controller and indicates that the DMA cycle requested by DRQ has been granted. $\overline{DACK}$ serves as the chip select input when data from screen memory is being loaded into the 8275 row buffers.

CCLK is the Character rate Clock used to time all of the internal operations of the 8275. This clock signal must be derived from external dot timing logic. Thus it is not truly a microprocessor system interface signal, but is associated more with the video and character generator logic. Nonetheless, we have grouped it with the other microprocessor interface signals since it is the primary timing input to the 8275 device.

V_{CC} and GND are the standard power (+5 volts) and ground connections.

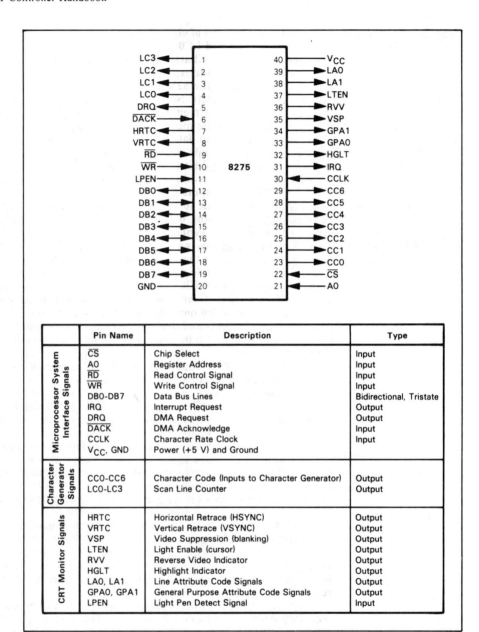

Figure 3-2. 8275 CRT Controller Pins and Signals

Character Generator Signals

There are two sets of signals associated directly with character generator logic: CC0-CC6 and LC0-LC3.

CC0-CC6 are the Character Code Outputs from the 8275 which will be used as inputs to character generator logic. The 7-bit character codes are simply the contents of the 8275's internal character row buffers and typically represent ASCII characters. Note that you load the internal row buffers with 8-bit data characters from memory but only output 7-bit character codes; the most significant bit of the memory data word is used to differentiate between special control codes and data for display and is not output on the character code lines. The most significant bit of data that is to be displayed must be set to 0. With the remaining 7-bit character codes you can represent 128 different characters. These are typically address inputs to the character generator.

The LC0-LC3 outputs are scan line counter signals which are used by character generator logic to select the proper dot pattern for the particular scan line currently being output. These are typically additional address inputs to the character generator.

CRT Monitor Signals

The 8275 provides an abundance of CRT monitor-related signals. Some of these signals are the familiar ones we have encountered and discussed in previous chapters, while others are unique, special-purpose signals. Let us begin with the standard CRT monitor signals.

HRTC and VRTC are the Horizontal and Vertical Retrace signals which, in more standard nomenclature, are usually named Horizontal Synchronization (HSYNC) and Vertical Synchronization (VSYNC). The duration of both of these signal pulses is programmable and is established using the Reset command.

VSP is the Video Suppression or blanking output that external logic can use to blank the video signal to the CRT monitor. The primary function of this signal is to suppress video during horizontal and vertical retrace operations, and it is automatically set high by the 8275 during these intervals. There are several other programmable functions for this signal which we shall discuss further when we describe the CRT monitor interface.

LTEN is the Light Enable signal which can be used to override character generator logic and present a continuous stream of dots to the CRT monitor. The primary function of this signal is to produce a cursor symbol at a programmed position on the screen. The signal can also be used in conjunction with special visual attribute codes to produce graphic (non-alphanumeric) symbols.

RVV is the Reverse Video signal which can be used by external logic to cause an inversion of the normal video signal. The result of this inversion is that a white character on a black background is displayed as a black character on a white background. You can also specify a reverse video cursor block instead of an underscore cursor: the RVV signal would be used to produce the reverse video symbol.

HGLT is the Highlight output signal which can be used by external logic to produce a dual-intensity display. The 8275 outputs HGLT high at screen positions that you specify under program control. It is then up to external logic or CRT monitor electronics to intensify the electron beam at those points on the screen.

LA0 and LA1 are Line Attribute signals which can be decoded by external logic to generate a set of predefined horizontal and vertical line combinations to produce a limited set of 11 graphic symbols. These two signals are automatically activated by the 8275 when one of the special control codes is read from screen memory.

GPA0 and GPA1 are General Purpose Attribute signals which can be used by external logic to generate special graphic symbols beyond those provided by the LA0 and LA1 codes. Since these signals have no predetermined functions, you can also use them for other system control functions. These signals are also activated automatically by the 8275 when appropriate control codes are read from screen memory.

LPEN is the Light Pen detect input signal which, in conjunction with exernal logic, can be used to implement a light pen circuit. A positive edge on the LPEN input causes the 8275 to capture and store the present row and column screen position information that it maintains in its internal counters.

As you can see from the preceding paragrahs, many of the CRT monitor interface signals require external logic in order to perform the function that they are intended for. We shall describe in some detail how these functions might be implemented later in this chapter when we discuss the CRT monitor interface. We will also see that many of these signals could be used to implement functions other than those indicated by their names, since all you are really doing is turning the signals on and off under program control at specified screen positions.

THE 8275 CRT CONTROLLER PROGRAMMABLE REGISTERS

The 8275 provides a number of internal registers which can be accessed under program control to direct the operation of the device and to obtain information from the device concerning its operation. The 8275 registers are illustrated in Figure 3-3.

The three primary register types are Status, Command, and Parameter. The $\overline{A0}$, $\overline{RD}$, $\overline{WR}$, and $\overline{CS}$ signals determine which register will be accessed. The conditions for accessing these registers are listed in Table 3-1. The Status register is a read-only register, the Command register is a write-only register, while some of the Parameter registers are read-only and others are write-only. **The Command and Status registers can be directly accessed by the microprocessor at any time, but the Parameter registers can only be accessed as part of a command sequence.** The Parameter registers are, effectively, a secondary set of internal registers. To access these secondary registers, you must first write a command byte into the Command register and then follow that command with read or write operations directed to the desired secondary registers.

We will defer a discussion of the individual bit assignments of the Command register and the secondary set of registers until we discuss the 8275 commands in detail. **At this point, we will limit our discussion to the individual bit assignments of the Status register.**

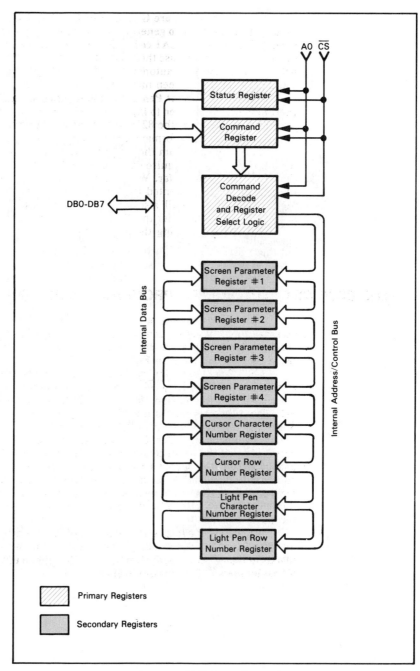

Figure 3-3. CRT Controller Registers

Table 3-1. 8275 Register Select Logic

$\overline{CS}$	A0	$\overline{RD}/\overline{WR}$	Register Accessed
L	H	$\overline{RD}$	Status
L	H	$\overline{WR}$	Command
L	L	$\overline{RD}$	Parameter Reg.
L	L	$\overline{WR}$	Parameter Reg.
H	X	X	—none—

Status
Register

Figure 3-4 shows the bit assignments for the 8275 Status register. The Status register is a read-only register and its contents can be read by the microprocessor at any time.

Status register bit 0 is the FIFO (first-in-first-out) Overrun bit. In addition to the two 80-character row buffers provided by the 8275, there are two internal 16-character FIFO registers. These FIFOs are used when you assign special attributes to character fields within a row and want to have that assignment or control code be invisible. If you attempt to assign more than 16 of these invisible field attribute control characters to a single character row, then bit 0 of the Status register will be set. We will give a fuller discussion of the invisible field attributes later in this chapter when we describe screen composition definitions. Bit 0 of a Status register will be reset when you perform a read of the Status register contents.

Bit 1 of the Status register is the DMA Underrun bit, and will be set to 1 if a DMA transfer requested by the 8275 has not been completed within the allotted time. (You specify under program control the time between DMA requests; if a preceding request has not been acknowledged by the time the next request is made, a DMA underrun condition exists.) The DMA underrun bit is reset whenever you read the contents of the Status register.

Bit 2 of the Status register is the Video Enable bit and will be set whenever the video operation of the CRT is enabled. This bit is set by issuing the Start Display command to the 8275 and is reset by issuing a Stop Display or Reset command.

Bit 3 of the Status register is the Improper Command bit and indicates that an error was made when issuing a command to the 8275. If you issue or attempt to read an incorrect number of parameter bytes (either too few or too many) following a command, this bit is set. The Improper Command bit is automatically reset after you read the contents of the Status register.

Status register bit 4 is the Light Pen Input bit and is set when a negative-to-positive transition is detected on the LPEN input to the 8275. Since detection of the LPEN input transition does not generate an interrupt, the microprocessor must check the state of Status register bit 4 to determine whether the LPEN signal has been detected. This bit is reset after you read the contents of the Status register.

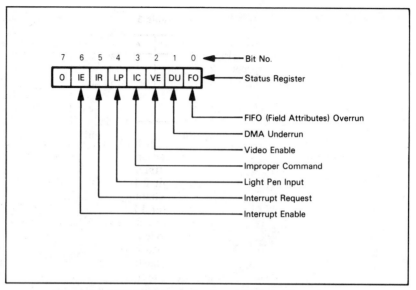

Figure 3-4. 8275 CRT Controller Status Register Bit Assignments

Bit 5 of the Status register is the Interrupt Request bit and will be set, if you have enabled interrupts, when display of the last character row of a frame is begun. This bit is set at the same time that the IRQ output signal goes high and is reset after you read the contents of the Status register.

Bit 6 of the Status register is the Interrupt Enable bit and indicates whether the 8275 will generate interrupts at the end of each frame. Interrupts are automatically enabled, and this bit is set, when you issue the Start Display command to the 8275. There are also separate Enable Interrupt and Disable Interrupt commands that can be used to manipulate this bit. In addition, the Interrupt Enable bit will be cleared and interrupts disabled when you issue a Reset command to the 8275.

Bit 7 of the Status register is not used and will always be 0 when you read the contents of the Status register.

THE 8275-MICROPROCESSOR SYSTEM INTERFACE

Since the 8275 device was originally designed to operate within a system using direct memory access (DMA), we will discuss the 8275-microprocessor system interface from this aspect. But it is not essential that a DMA device be utilized for 8275 support. A design example in which a microprocessor fully supports the 8275 is given by Intel in Application Note AP-62. In that application note, an external PROM is used to produce the DMA-type handshake signals needed to load data into the 8275's row buffers. Regardless of whether you use a standard DMA controller device or provide other external logic to implement that function, the timing sequences we describe in the following paragraphs will still apply.

Figure 3-5 shows, in a simplified form, the relationship between the 8275 device, a DMA controller, a microprocessor, and system memory. The 8275 communicates with the microprocessor to obtain command and parameter information and to pass status and parameter information back to the microprocessor. Transfers of data for display on the CRT screen go from screen memory to the 8275 under the control of the DMA controller. Let us first look at communications between the microprocessor and the 8275.

Microprocessor Interface

When the microprocessor needs to issue commands and parameters to the 8275 or to read the contents of the 8275 Status register, it simply accesses the device using a standard I/O read or I/O write operation. The timing for these transactions is quite straightforward. Timing for a write operation which would be used to issue a command to the 8275 or load a parameter into one of the internal 8275 registers can be illustrated as follows:

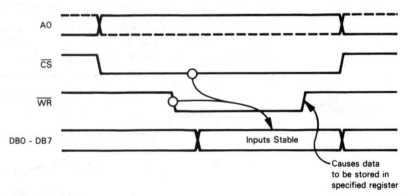

The Chip Select ($\overline{\text{CS}}$) signal must be low, the A0 register select input must be stable, and the data that is to be written into the selected register must be valid before the write ($\overline{\text{WR}}$) signal returns high. This timing is the same as that which would be used with any I/O port or memory device.

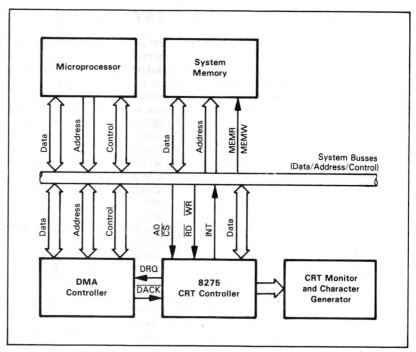

Figure 3-5. 8275 CRT Controller Functional Position in a Microprocessor System

A register read operation which would be used by the microprocessor to obtain status or parameter information from the 8275 device is equally straightforward and can be illustrated as follows:

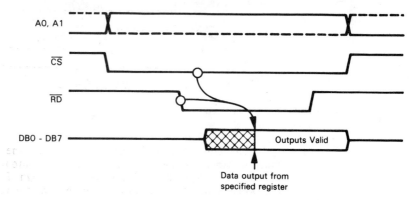

DMA Controller
Interface

Most communications between the microprocessor and the 8275 will take place at system startup when you establish such initial values as screen format, data transfer modes and so on. The microprocessor must also access the 8275 directly to move the cursor and to initiate and terminate display. **The bulk of system involvement with the 8275,** however, will be in transferring data that is to be displayed on the screen from system (screen) memory to the CRT controller. This activity **can proceed with almost no microprocessor involvement and is conducted by interaction between the DMA controller and the 8275. System activity during this DMA transfer of display data from memory to the CRT controller can be illustrated as follows:**

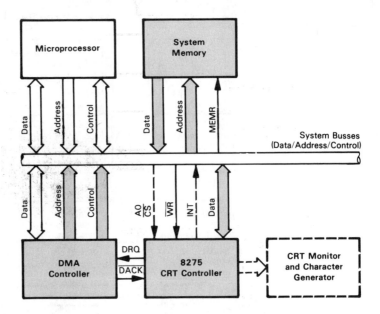

As the 8275 requires data for its character row buffers, it generates DMA requests by setting its DRQ signal high. The DMA controller responds by gaining control of the system busses, reading a byte of data from system memory (using $\overline{\text{MEMR}}$), and simultaneously writing that byte into the 8275's character row buffer (using $\overline{\text{IOW}}$). **The timing for this DMA transfer of data can be illustrated as follows:**

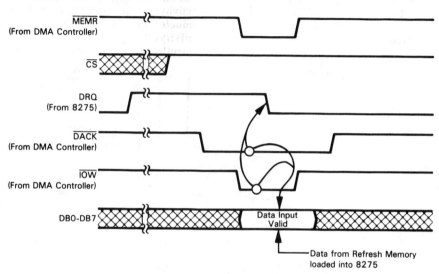

The 8275 DMA Request (DRQ) signal is reset when the $\overline{\text{DACK}}$ and $\overline{\text{WR}}$ signals are received back from the DMA controller. This combination of signals loads the byte of data being presented to the 8275 on its DB0-DB7 pins into the character row buffer. Note that the Chip Select ($\overline{\text{CS}}$) input into the 8275 remains high during DMA operations. This is logical, since the address information on the system busses, which would normally be used to generate the $\overline{\text{CS}}$ signal, contains screen memory addresses during these DMA cycles. Thus the $\overline{\text{DACK}}$ signal performs the chip select function during DMA operations.

The preceding illustration showed the transfer of a single byte of data from memory to the 8275. These DMA cycles must, of course, be repeated frequently to load and reload the character row buffers as data is sent to the CRT monitor. **You have two options in implementing these DMA cycles. One option is to perform data transfers on a byte-by-byte basis with each DMA cycle being individually initiated. This mode of operation can be illustrated as follows:**

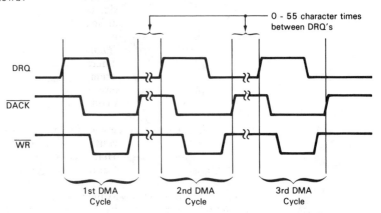

Burst Mode

As the 8275 requires a byte of data for its character row buffer, it sets the DRQ signal high and the DMA controller supplies the requested data. You specify the interval between DMA cycles as one of the Reset command parameters. **The alternate mode of DMA operation is to operate in a burst mode where several bytes of data are transferred to the 8275 in response to a single request. The timing for this mode of operation can be illustrated as follows:**

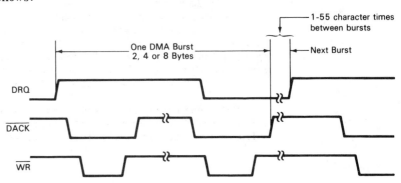

Here the 8275 sets the DRQ signal high and keeps it high until the DMA controller has transferred either 2, 4, or 8 bytes of data from screen memory. Of course, the DMA controller you are using must be capable of responding to this continuous DMA request. The 8257 and 8237 DMA controllers, which the 8275 was designed to operate with, operate in this burst mode.

The DMA mode of operation that you use will depend on the needs of your system. The ability to program the 8275 so that it can operate in either single cycle or burst mode, combined with flexible spacing between DMA operations, gives you great flexibility in fitting the bus access requirements of the 8275 into your system.

The DMA timing signals that we have illustrated are only those which directly affect the 8275. There will, of course, be a number of other signals exchanged within the system to obtain control of the bus and to read data from memory. Since these signals will be determined by the particular microprocessor and DMA controller you are using, they are beyond the scope of our discussion here.

There are two aspects of the DMA operation that we have not yet discussed: how the DMA controller obtains the starting address for screen memory accesses, and what the timing relationships are between DMA operations and display of data on the CRT screen.

The DMA controller must receive the screen memory starting address from the microprocessor as part of the system initialization operation. Then, when the 8275 makes its first DMA request, the DMA controller reads the first byte of data that is to be displayed from screen memory, and transfers it to the 8275's character row buffer. After each access of screen memory, the DMA controller must increment its address counter so that when the next DMA request is received, the next character in screen memory will be accessed. The DMA controller will simply continue to increment the screen memory addresses as each DMA request is received from the 8275 until all of the data that is to be displayed on the screen has been read from memory and sent to the 8275. At that point, the DMA controller must once again be given the starting address for screen memory, since it would otherwise simply continue incrementing its address counter. **The 8275** handles this situation by generating an interrupt when display of the last row of characters on the screen is begun. This **interrupt can be used to inform the microprocessor that it must once again reload the DMA controller address register with the starting address of screen memory in preparation for display of the next frame of data.**

DMA operations can proceed continuously while data is only being sent to the CRT monitor by the 8275 because of the dual character row buffers. Let us look now at how these row buffers operate.

Internal
Character
Buffers

     The two internal recirculating buffers provided by the 8275 can each hold up to 80 bytes of data. While one buffer is being loaded from refresh memory under the control of the DMA controller, the contents of the other buffer are being recirculated and presented to external character generator logic as each scan line of a character row is sent to the CRT monitor. **Obviously, the first character buffer must be filled before the first character row of data on the screen is to be displayed. The first DMA request of a frame is generated by the 8275 one character-row time before the end of vertical retrace.** (Vertical retrace is program specified to be from one to four character rows in duration.) Thus during this last character-row time of vertical retrace, the first character row buffer is being filled. **This can be illustrated as follows:**

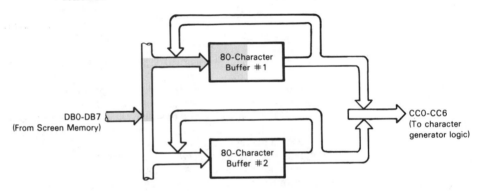

     You have one character-row time (from one to sixteen horizontal-scan-line times) in which to fill the character buffer. Display of the contents of that character buffer then commences with the contents of the buffer being presented to character generator logic via the CC0-CC6 outputs. Meanwhile, character buffer #2 is being filled using DMA from screen memory as shown in the following illustration:

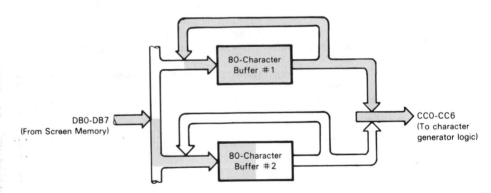

When all of the scan lines comprising the first character row have been sent to the CRT monitor, the contents of character buffer #2 will be connected to the CC0-CC6 pins for the second character row of the screen, while buffer #1 is being refilled from screen memory with the new data that will comprise the third character row. This can be illustrated as follows:

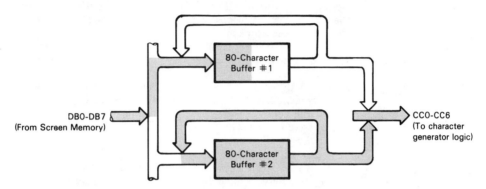

DB0-DB7
(From Screen Memory)

80-Character Buffer #1

80-Character Buffer #2

CC0-CC6
(To character generator logic)

This switching back and forth between character row buffers continues until all character rows of a frame have been completed. DMA will then cease during vertical retrace until one character-row time before the beginning of the next frame. The cycle we have just described will then be repeated. **Note that the 8275 controls the switching back and forth between the two characer row buffers; this operation is transparent as far as the microprocessor system is concerned.** The system need only guarantee that the DMA rate is sufficient to finish loading each row buffer in the time required to present the preceding character row to the CRT monitor.

THE 8275-CHARACTER GENERATOR INTERFACE

The logic provided by the 8275 to interface to character generator logic consists of three groups of signals: LC0-LC3, CC0-CC6, and LA0, LA1. The two signals LA0, LA1 which are more closely related to creation of the video signal, come into play if you utilize the limited built-in graphics capability of the 8275. Let us begin with the more straightforward aspects of the character generator logic.

The Character Code outputs (CC0-CC6) and Line Count outputs (LC0-LC3) will be used as address inputs to character generator logic. (For a complete discussion of character generator logic, refer to Chapter 1.) CC0-CC6 are simply the outputs from the 8275's internal character row buffer. This row buffer is recirculated at the Character Clock (CCLK) rate during each scan line so that the code for each character position on the scan line is output to the character generator. The timing for these Character Code outputs is shown in Figure 3-6.

The internal character row buffer contents are shifted at the Character Clock (CCLK) rate to present the appropriate character code outputs to the character generator logic. Since the character row buffer can contain from two to eighty characters (you specify the number of characters under program control), the number of times the row buffer will be shifted per scan line will be from 2 to 80. After the last character has been output to the character generator logic, recirculation of the row buffer continues during horizontal retrace but VSP goes active to blank any meaningless video information.

Scan Line Counter Modes

The scan line counter outputs (LC0-LC3) to the character generator logic are held steady during each horizontal scan line while the character codes are being output. Upon completion of each scan line, the line counter outputs are incremented to address the next line of dots for the character codes that will be output. The 8275 scan line counter has two modes of operation: in Mode 0 the output of the line counter is the same as the scan line number of the character row, while in Mode 1 the counter is offset by 1 from the line number. The counting progression that occurs for a character row in each of the two modes can be illustrated as follows:

Scan Line #		Mode 0	Mode 1	
0	O O O O O O O O	0000	1011	
1	O O O O ● O O O O	0001	0000	
2	O O O ● O ● O O O	0010	0001	
3	O O ● O O O ● O O	0011	0010	
4	O ● O O O O O ● O	0100	0011	
5	O ● O O O O O ● O	0101	0100	
6	O ● ● ● ● ● ● ● O	0110	0101	
7	O ● O O O O O ● O	0111	0110	
8	O ● O O O O O ● O	1000	0111	
9	O ● O O O O O ● O	1001	1000	
10	● ● ● ● ● ● ● ●	1010	1001	Underline in
11	O O O O O O O O	1011	1010	Scan Line #10

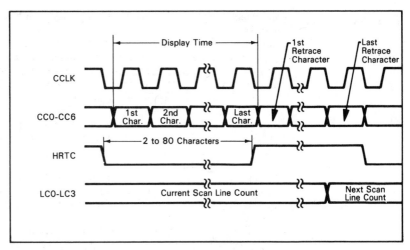

Figure 3-6. 8275 Character Code Output Timing

In Mode 0, the line count output during the first scan line (line number 0) will always be 0000. In Mode 1, however, the line count output during the first scan line will be the maximum line count that you have specified, and the count will then go to 0000 for scan line number 1. You specify the line counter mode of operation you desire under program control as part of the Reset command. The mode you select will depend on the type of character generator you are using. For example, if a character generator expects a line count address of 1 for the first row of dots, you might use Mode 0 so that an address of all zeros would not select the character generator, but instead would produce the line of dots used for inter-character row spacing. Similarly, if a character generator expects a line count address of zero to access the first row of dots, then you might use line counter Mode 1.

Graphic Capabilities

Let us now look at the limited capabilities provided by the 8275 via the Line Attribute (LA0-LA1) signals.

Character Attribute Codes

The line attribute signals are manipulated by writing special character attribute codes to the 8275. You do not have to issue special commands to the 8275 in order to manipulate the line attribute outputs; you simply store the special character codes in screen memory. You will recall that data in screen memory consists of 8-bit bytes. Normal data codes have the most significant bit set to 0. If the 8275 receives a byte of data from screen memory with the most significant bit set to 1, it recognizes this as some type of control code. There are three types of control codes: character attribute codes which cause the line attribute outputs to be manipulated; field attribute codes which affect the visual characteristics of a group of characters that are to be displayed;

and special codes which affect DMA and screen blanking. At this point, we will limit our discussion to the character attribute codes. The format for the character attribute codes is as follows:

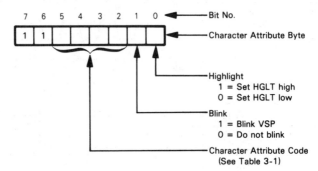

Bits 7 and 6 of the character attribute byte must both be set to 1. Bits 0 and 1 can be set to manipulate the Highlight (HGLT) signal and to cause the character to blink by manipulating the Video Suppression (VSP) signal. We shall discuss the highlight and blink functions later when we describe the interface to the CRT monitor. Let us now concentrate on the character attribute codes which are contained in bits 5 through 2 of the byte.

Table 3-2 describes the effects of the various character attribute codes on the LA1, LA0, VSP and LTEN output signals and also indicates the resultant symbols which can be created. Creation of these symbols requires the use of very specific external logic. The logic you must provide is illustrated in Figure 3-7. The shift register shown in the figure is a 9-bit parallel-to-serial shift register, and thus each character space in this example would be 9 dots in width. When LA0 and LA1 are both output high from the 8275, five 1's would be loaded into the least significant bits of the shift register and four 0's would be loaded into the four most significant bits of the shift register. When the contents of the shift register are shifted out serially and sent to the CRT monitor, a horizontal line is produced on the left half of the character space. Similarly, when LA0 is low and LA1 is high, this causes a horizontal line on the right half of the character space to be produced. When LA1 is low and LA0 is high, a 1 bit is loaded only into the center bit of the shift register, and 0's are loaded in the four least significant and four most significant bits of the shift register. If this is repeated for all scan lines comprising the character, a vertical line down the center of the character position is produced. Vertical line segments on the upper or lower half of a character space are produced by setting LA1 low and LA0 high for every scan line on the character row, and then activating the Video Suppression (VSP) signal during those scan lines above or below the underline position. When VSP is high, it disables the output from the shift register via the NOR gate, so that no dots are sent to the CRT monitor.

Table 3-2. 8275 CRT Controller Character Attribute Codes and Resultant Symbols

Character Attribute Code		Outputs				Symbol	Description
Bits 5432	For Scan Lines	LA1	LA0	VSP	LTEN		
0000	Above Underline	0	0	1	0	⌐	Top Left Corner
	Underline	1	0	0	0		
	Below Underline	0	1	0	0		
0001	Above Underline	0	0	1	0	⌐	Top Right Corner
	Underline	1	1	0	0		
	Below Underline	0	1	0	0		
0010	Above Underline	0	1	0	0	L	Bottom Left Corner
	Underline	1	0	0	0		
	Below Underline	0	0	1	0		
0011	Above Underline	0	1	0	0	⌐	Bottom Right Corner
	Underline	1	1	0	0		
	Below Underline	0	0	1	0		
0100	Above Underline	0	0	1	0	T	Top Intersect
	Underline	0	0	0	1		
	Below Underline	0	1	0	0		
0101	Above Underline	0	1	0	0	⊣	Right Intersect
	Underline	1	1	0	0		
	Below Underline	0	1	0	0		
0110	Above Underline	0	1	0	0	⊢	Left Intersect
	Underline	1	0	0	0		
	Below Underline	0	1	0	0		
0111	Above Underline	0	1	0	0	⊥	Bottom Intersect
	Underline	0	0	0	1		
	Below Underline	0	0	1	0		
1000	Above Underline	0	0	1	0	—	Horizontal Line
	Underline	0	0	0	1		
	Below Underline	0	0	1	0		
1001	Above Underline	0	1	0	0	|	Vertical Line
	Underline	0	1	0	0		
	Below Underline	0	1	0	0		
1010	Above Underline	0	1	0	0	+	Crossed Lines
	Underline	0	0	0	1		
	Below Underline	0	1	0	0		
1011	Above Underline	0	0	0	0		Not Recommended*
	Underline	0	0	0	0		
	Below Underline	0	0	0	0		
1100	Above Underline	0	0	1	0		Special Codes
	Underline	0	0	1	0		
	Below Underline	0	0	1	0		
1101	Above Underline Underline Below Underline		Undefined				Illegal
1110	Above Underline Underline Below Underline		Undefined				Illegal
1111	Above Underline Underline Below Underline		Undefined				Illegal

* Character Attribute Code 1011 is not recommended for normal operation. Since none of the attribute outputs are active, the character generator will not be disabled, and an indeterminate character will be generated.
Character Attribute Codes 1101, 1110, and 1111 are illegal.

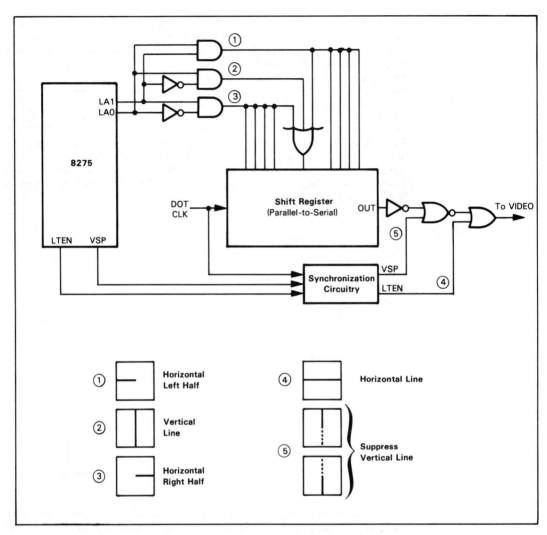

Figure 3-7. External Logic Required to Implement Graphics Provided by the 8275 CRT Controller

This is a good point to note that the symbols shown in Figure 3-1 imply that the horizontal and vertical line segments run through the center of a character space. This is not necessarily true: the position of the vertical line or line segments is determined by the bit position where you load the appropriate code-produced signals into the shift register. In Figure 3-7 we loaded the vertical line signal into the center bit of a 9-bit shift register and caused it to appear in the center of a character location. The horizontal lines or line segments will appear on only one scan line of the character row, and will be on the scan line where you have programmed the underline to be displayed. **The underline position is program-established using the Reset command and can be on any scan line within a character row. Thus, for example, if you have specified that the underline is to be displayed on line number 9 of a character row comprised of 12 scan lines, the first two symbols shown in Table 3-1 would appear as follows:**

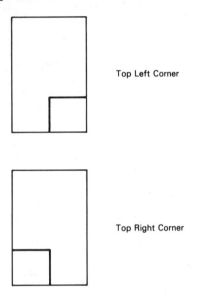

Top Left Corner

Top Right Corner

A horizontal line completely across a character location is produced using the Light Enable (LTEN) signal. Both the LA1 and LA0 outputs will be low during the creation of a complete horizontal line. The horizontal line will be produced on the scan line where you have specified that the underline is to appear.

We intentionally kept the logic shown in Figure 3-7 as simple as possible so that we could focus more clearly on the logic in our discussion. In actual use, however, additional logic would be required since the other character generator logic present in the system would utilize the same video shift register to produce the VIDEO signal. **The additional logic required to select between the line attribute-produced characters and standard character generator logic is shown in Figure 3-8.** A NOR gate is used to disable the outputs from the character generator logic if either LA1 or LA0 is high. The inputs to the shift register are then from OR gates which have as their inputs the LA1/ LA0-produced signals or the outputs from the character generator logic.

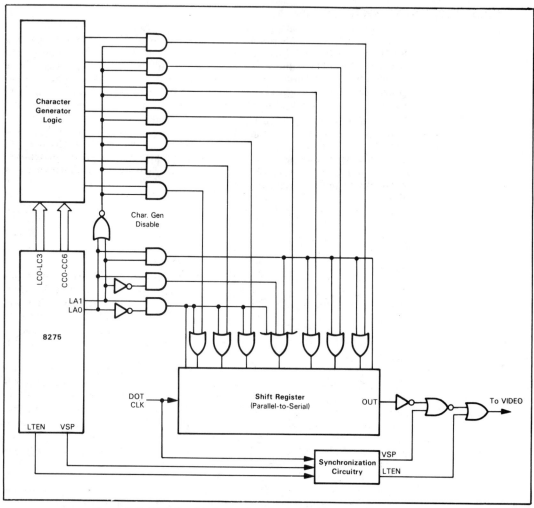

Figure 3-8. 8275 Graphic Logic Combined with Character Generator Logic

  While the logic required to implement the line attribute graphics of the 8275 is not complicated, it is still quite a bit of circuitry to simply produce eleven limited graphic characters. If some graphic capabilities are required, it may prove easier simply to utilize a character generator which can produce the required symbols.

Field Attribute Designations

The character attribute logic we have just described applies only to a single character position on the screen; when a character from screen memory contains 1's in the two most significant bit positions, it is interpreted by the 8275 as being a special character that affects that particular character location on the screen. The 8275 also recognizes Field Attribute Control bytes when read from screen memory. These bytes have the format shown in Figure 3-9.

Field   The Field Attribute Control byte is similar to the Character Attribute byte with the significant difference that it affects all data bytes which follow until another control byte is read from screen memory. Thus all the characters between these control bytes, the "field," will have the characteristics defined by the Field Attribute Control byte. The two least significant bits of the Field Attribute Control byte are the same as those of the character attribute codes which we described earlier: bit 0 causes HGLT to be set high or low, and bit 1 causes blinking by modulating the VSP signal at a frequency equal to the screen refresh frequency divided by 32. The difference is that both of these signals will be maintained as designated for an entire field until another control byte, or the end of the screen, is encountered.

Bits 2 and 3 of the Field Attribute Control byte can be used to manipulate the two General Purpose Attribute signals (GPA0, GPA1) of the 8275. The use of these two signals is entirely up to the system designer; they will simply be output at the designated levels until the next control byte is encountered. Some possible uses for these signals include control of colors in color CRT monitors or selection of alternate character generator logic to implement special characters within a field.

Bit 4 of the Field Attribute Control byte manipulates the RVV (Reverse Video) signal from the 8275, while bit 5 manipulates the LTEN (Light Enable) signal. While the signal names assigned to these two bits (and pins) imply very specific uses, they may also be put to general purpose use if your system requires it. The only limitation to using these two signals as general purpose signals is the fact that both may be used during creation of the cursor symbol, and the LTEN signal is also used during creation of the graphic symbols provided by the Character Attribute Codes.

The presumed purpose of the RVV and LTEN bits and signals is to cause the characters following the Field Attribute Code to be presented in reverse video (if RVV is high) and/or to be underlined (if LTEN is high).

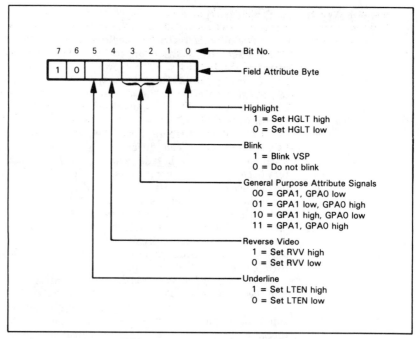

Figure 3-9. 8275 CRT Controller Field Attribute Control Byte

Visible/Invisible Field Attribute Control Codes

The 8275 provides you with two options with regard to the field attributes: the Field Attribute Control bytes read from screen memory can occupy a visible position on the screen, or they can be made invisible and simply affect the subsequent character field. You specify the desired mode as part of the Reset command. If you specify the visible field attribute mode, the Field Attribute Control bytes read from screen memory will occupy a position on the screen although they will appear as blanks, since the 8275 will automatically cause the Video Suppression (VSP) signal to be activated during that character position. The designated field attribute will then be activated after this blank character position. **This visible field attribute mode can be illustrated as follows:**

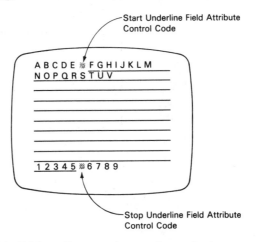

The visible field attribute mode may be perfectly acceptable in many applications where changes from one type of field to another are also accompanied by some space between fields. The acceptability of this mode will depend, to some extent, on how crowded the screen is and how critical this waste of screen space is to your application.

If you select the invisible field attribute mode for the 8275, then the internal First-In-First-Out (FIFOs) registers of the 8275 are activated. Each of the 8275's internal character row buffers has an associated 16-character FIFO. In this mode of operation, when a Field Attribute Control byte is loaded into a row buffer, the 8275 recognizes it as such and places the following data character in the FIFO. When the time comes to display that character row, the 8275 once again recognizes the Field Attribute Control byte before it is to be sent to the CRT monitor, and substitutes the appropriate following character byte from the FIFO on the Character Code outputs. Simultaneously, the 8275 activates the specified field attribute control signal(s). **An example of invisible field attributes can be illustrated as follows:**

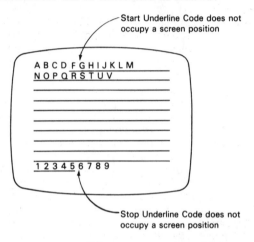

Several problems are introduced by the use of the Field Attribute Control bytes. First of all, whether you use the visible or invisible mode, the Field Attribute Control bytes will occupy locations in screen memory. Since the number of attribute control bytes per display row may vary, the fixed relationship between character positions on the screen and system memory address pointers to the beginning of the screen, beginning of row, etc., may no longer be constant. **Therefore system software required to keep track of screen locations will be complicated** since it must also keep track of the number of Field Attribute Control bytes in each row while pointer locations are being manipulated. **In addition, each Field Attribute Control byte increases the size of screen memory** since it occupies a location in that memory. **DMA transfers and character deletion or insertion routines may also be complicated** by the presence of Field Attribute Control bytes within data fields. **Finally, you must be aware that** since the 8275 stores the character which immediately follows a field attribute control byte in a FIFO, and subsequently outputs that following character to the CRT, **you cannot follow a Field Attribute Control byte with any of the character attribute bytes or other special codes that the 8275 would otherwise recognize.**

SPECIAL CONTROL CODES

In addition to the character attribute codes and field attribute control codes which we discussed earlier, the 8275 recognizes four additional special control characters which affect DMA operations and blanking of the screen. Just as with the character attribute and field attribute codes, these special control codes are simply placed in screen memory and are recognized by the 8275 as control codes because their most significant bit is set to 1. The format for these codes is illustrated in Figure 3-10.

The four most significant bits must be set to 1, bits 4 and 3 must be 0's, and the two least significant bits specify the control function.

End of Row Control Code

The End of Row code (00) causes the remainder of the current character row to be blanked. This is accomplished by setting the Video Suppression (VSP) signal high, and holding it high from that character position where the control code is located to the end of the character row. This is a very simple way of clearing a portion of a character row which would otherwise have to be done by writing the character code for blanks or spaces into the corresponding screen memory locations. One drawback of this code is that it applies from the point where it is detected to the end of the character row; you cannot just blank out the middle portion of a character row.

Stop DMA Control Code

The End of Row-Stop DMA code (01) affects the display in the same way as the End of Row code, and also causes the 8275 to stop generating DMA requests for the remainder of that character row. This combination makes a great deal of sense, since if you are not going to display data beyond the End of Row code, there would be no reason why you would still want to access data from screen memory. You thus reduce the DMA demand on the system busses.

End of Screen Control Code

The End of Screen code (10) has the same effect as the End of Row code but it applies for all characters from the point of encounter until the end of the frame. Once again the VSP signal is used to perform the blanking operation.

The End of Screen-Stop DMA code (11) affects the display in the same way as the End of Screen code and also causes the 8275 to cease generating DMA requests for the remainder of the frame. Thus you can blank all of the screen, from the point where the code is encountered to the end of the screen, with a single control code, instead of writing all spaces into the appropriate positions in screen memory.

If you do not use the Stop DMA feature with the End of Row or End of Screen codes, DMA requests will continue to be generated by the 8275 for the remainder of the row or screen. The characters read from screen memory, however, are simply ignored by the 8275. The exception is that after an End of Row character, the 8275 will still recognize and respond to an End of Screen character. After an End of Screen character, however, all subsequent characters will be ignored.

If the Stop DMA features are used, there will be a one character delay before DMA requests will be terminated since the 8275 will have already begun to access the next character when it is recognizing the Stop DMA code. Thus a dummy character must be placed in screen memory after the Stop DMA character. The exception is if the Stop DMA code is the last character in a burst or in a character row; in this case, no additional DMA requests will be generated.

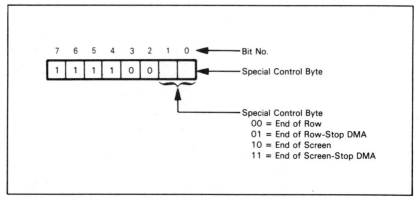

Figure 3-10. 8275 Special Control Code Byte Format

THE 8275-CRT MONITOR INTERFACE

Figure 3-11 illustrates the signals provided by the 8275 to implement the interface to a CRT monitor. Only two of the signals (HRTC, VRTC) are absolutely essential to the CRT monitor interface; the other signals represent special options provided by the 8275, and their implementation will be application-dependent.

HRTC (Horizontal Retrace) and VRTC (Vertical Retrace) are the standard HSYNC and VSYNC signals which we have previously discussed. The frequency and pulse intervals of both of these signals are programmable and are specified as part of the Reset command.

The RVV (Reverse Video), VSP (Video Suppression), and LTEN (Light Enable) signals can all be combined with the output from the video shift register to produce different visual effects on the screen. As we discussed earlier, these signals are sometimes manipulated directly while Character Attribute or Field Attribute control bytes are read from screen memory; the signals are also manipulated by the 8275 to create the cursor. If you compare the external logic required to create the cursor for the 8275 to that which we described for the DP8350 in Chapter 2, you will see that the logic here is slightly simplified. The DP8350 provided no reverse video signal and you had to perform that function externally. The 8275, on the other hand, allows you to specify a reversed cursor if you so desire, and activates the RVV signal if you have so specified. Thus you are sacrificing one pin on the 8275 to implement this function (although, of course, it is also used to create reverse video characters or entire fields of characters; its use is not limited only to the cursor symbol).

The HGLT (Highlight) signal is automatically set high or low by the 8275 as specified by control bytes read from display memory. The use of this signal is completely application-dependent and is not involved with creation of the cursor or the character attribute code graphic capabilities of the 8275. HGLT will simply be set high or low as specified for an entire character field.

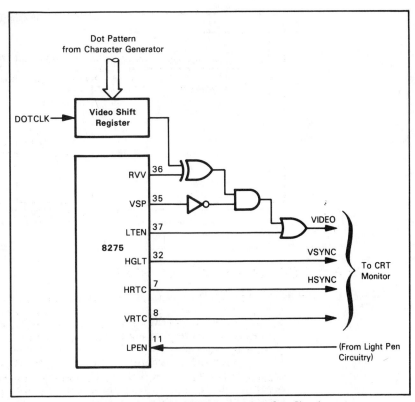

Figure 3-11. 8275 CRT Monitor Interface Signals

The **LPEN (Light Pen) input to the 8275 requires a negative-to-positive transition from external circuitry to cause the controller to store its current character and row counter values in its internal Light Pen registers.** You can then read the contents of the Light Pen registers by issuing the appropriate command to the 8275. Because of the delays inherent in external light pen circuitry, the values stored in the light pen Character Count register will be offset by at least three characters from the actual position where the light pen was physically positioned on the screen. Therefore, your software will have to adjust this value accordingly.

Table 3-3. 8275 CRT Controller Command Summary

Command	Command Byte		Number of Parameter Bytes (Note 1)	Command Byte (Hex)
	(MSB) ← Bit Format → (LSB)			
	765	43210		
Reset	000	00000	4W	00_{16}
Start Display	001	Note 2	—	Note 2
Stop Display	010	00000	—	40_{16}
Read Light Pen	011	00000	2R	50_{16}
Load Cursor Registers	100	00000	2W	80_{16}
Enable Interrupt	101	00000	—	$A0_{16}$
Disable Interrupt	110	00000	—	$B0_{16}$
Preset Counters	111	00000	—	$D0_{16}$

1. The least significant 5 bits of Start Display Command determine DMA rate.
2. W = Write to 8275, R = Read from 8275.

THE 8275 CRT CONTROLLER COMMANDS

Table 3-3 shows the bit format for each of the eight commands that the 8275 will respond to. Any of the commands can be issued at any time to the 8275; you simply perform a write operation ($\overline{WR}$ low) to the device with the A0 input high and $\overline{CS}$ input low. The command byte is then input to the 8275 on the D7-D0 pins. The three most significant bits of the command byte determine the command that will be executed. The five least significant bits are set to 0 for all but the Start Display command. Three of the commands have parameter bytes associated with them: the Reset and Load Cursor Register commands require that you write additional parameter bytes to the 8275 after the command byte, while the Read Light Pen command requires that you read two bytes from the 8275 after issuing the command. If a command has parameters associated with it, these parameters must be transferred before another command is issued.

The Reset command is the most complicated to describe, since it is used to define a number of basic operating characteristics for the 8275. Let us therefore begin our command descriptions with it.

The 8275 Reset Command

Figure 3-12 shows the format for the Reset command byte and the four parameter bytes which must follow the command. The Reset command must be issued to the 8275 whenever the system is first initialized, since it determines many of the basic operating characteristics of the 8275. The command can also be re-issued while the device is operating to change certain operating characteristics. While some of the characteristics, such as vertical retrace time, would not normally be changed once established at system powerup, others such as cursor format or underline placement might be altered depending on the data that was to be displayed for a given application.

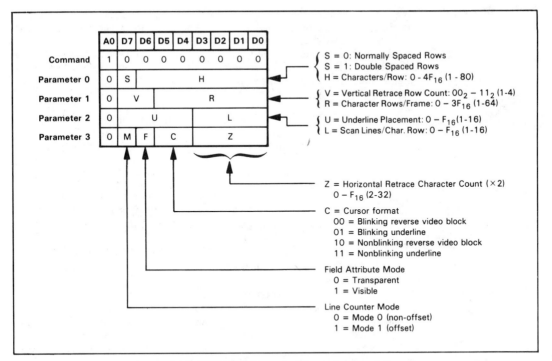

Figure 3-12. 8275 CRT Controller Reset Command Format

The command byte of the Reset command simply consists of all zeros and must be followed by writing four parameter bytes.

The seven least significant bits of the first parameter byte specify the number of characters that are to be displayed on each row. The allowable range is from 1 to 80 ($0-50_{16}$). Although the seven bits could be used to specify values as great as 127 ($7F_{16}$), values greater than 80 are invalid since that is the maximum capacity of the 8275's character row buffers.

The most significant bit of the first parameter byte specifies either normal spacing or double spacing of character rows. In normal spacing, the only separation between adjacent character rows is the one or two scan lines at the top or bottom of each character row which are not used in formation of the characters. If you specify double spacing, however, each character row is separated by a complete row of blank characters. The 8275 accomplishes this by repeating the row but activating VSP for the entire row. During the blanked row DMA activity is not needed, thus it is not requested.

The second parameter byte of the Reset command specifies the number of character rows per frame and the time allotted to the vertical retrace operation. The six least significant bits specify the number of character rows per frame in the range of 1- 64 (0-3F$_{16}$). Upon completion of display of the last specified character row on the screen, the Vertical Retrace (VRTC) signal is set high to indicate the beginning of the vertical retrace operation. The duration of the high level of the VRTC signal is specified using the two most significant bits of the second parameter byte. The VRTC signal will remain true for an integral number of character row times from 1 to 4. We should note that while you can program the duration of a true level of the VRTC pulse, you have no freedom in positioning the VRTC pulse; it goes true at the end of the last display row, and is set low again at the end of the last retrace row just prior to the beginning of the first displayable row of the next frame. This provides less flexibility than the DP8350 which we described in Chapter 2. Accordingly, some external circuitry may be needed to generate a VSYNC pulse of a proper duration for the CRT monitor.

The third parameter byte of the Reset command specifies the number of scan lines that comprises the character row, and the placement of an underline or cursor on a scan line within a character row. You can specify that a character row be comprised of from 1 to 16 scan lines. Thus this specification combined with the character rows per frame specification of the second parameter byte determines the total number of displayable scan lines per frame. The most significant four bits of the third parameter byte allow you to position the scan line within a character row where the LTEN signal should be activated to create an underline. You can specify that the underline be in any of the scan lines from 1 to 16 on the character row. **There are several rules that apply to this underline placement specification:**

· If the line number you specify for the underline is greater than seven, both the first and last scan lines of the character row will automatically be blanked (VSP high) by the 8275.

· If the line number specified for the underline is less than or equal to seven, the first and last scan lines of the character row will not be blanked.

· If the line number specified for the underline is greater than the maximum number of scan lines per character row (specified in the least significant four bits of this parameter byte), then the underline will not appear at all.

The fourth parameter byte of the Reset command specifies four different operating characteristics for the 8275: HRTC duration, cursor format, field attribute mode, and line counter mode. The four least significant bits specify, in increments of two character counts (or CCLK periods), **the duration of the horizontal retrace (HRTC) pulse.** HRTC will be set high after the last character time of a scan line and will remain high for a duration of from 2 to 32 CCLK periods. Just as with the VRTC specification, you have no positioning control of the HSYNC pulse within the horizontal retrace time. If additional shaping or positioning of the HSYNC pulse is required, then external circuitry must be used to interface to the CRT monitor.

Bits 5 and 4 of the fourth parameter byte specify the format of the cursor that will be displayed at the character location specified by the contents of the Cursor register. There are four options: the cursor can consist of either an underline on the scan line specified for underline placement in the third parameter byte, or it can be presented as a reverse video block symbol. The reverse block cursor symbol is created by activating the RVV signal at the specified cursor character location. In addition, either the single underline or the reverse block cursor symbol can be made to blink; the blinking is accomplished by modulating the VSP output from the 8275 at a frequency equal to the frame refresh rate divided by 32.

Bit 6 of the fourth parameter byte specifies whether field attribute characters are to occupy a position on the screen or whether they are to be made transparent by utilizing the 8275's FIFOs. The most significant bit of the fourth parameter byte specifies the scan line counter mode. The scan line counter modes and field attribute control character modes have been described in the preceding sections of this chapter and we shall not discuss them further at this point.

The 8275 Start and Stop Display Commands

Figure 3-13 shows the format for the Start Display command. This command requires no subsequent parameter bytes, but does include some additional control information in the least significant five bits of the command byte. The Start Display command would normally follow the Reset command since, in addition to determining the DMA rate that will be used, it enables the video-related outputs (by setting VSP low) of the 8275 and sets the Interrupt Enable and Video Enable status bits in the 8275's Status register. The DMA rate characteristics are defined in the least significant five bits of the command byte; we discussed and illustrated the DMA burst count and burst space timing earlier in this chapter when we discussed the controller-to-microprocessor interface. You should refer to that discussion for timing illustrations.

The Stop Display command simply causes the Video Suppression (VSP) signal to be set high, and it remains high until you issue a Start Display command to the 8275. The other video-related outputs, including HRTC, VRTC, LC0-LC3, and CC0-CC6, all continue to run despite the Stop Display command. It is just the high level of the VSP output that must be used to disable presentation of video to the CRT monitor. The Video Enable status flag is reset, however, so that the microprocessor can determine the state of the video-related outputs of the 8275. The Start Display command must be issued to reenable these video-related outputs. There are no parameter bytes required in conjunction with the Stop Display command; you simply write the command byte of 40_{16} to the 8275 with A0 set to 1.

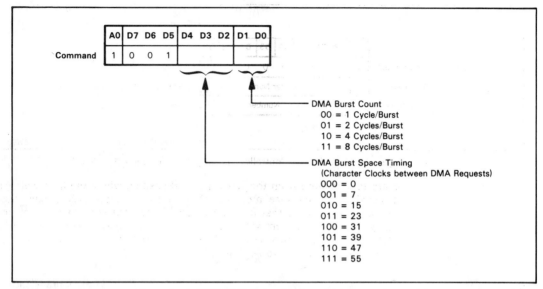

Figure 3-13. 8275 CRT Controller Start Display Command

The 8275 Preset Counter Command

The Preset Counter command ($E0_{16}$) causes the 8275's internal character counter and line counter to be preset to a value corresponding to a screen display position at the top left corner. It requires two character clock (CCLK) periods to complete the preset operation. The counters will be held in this preset state until you issue another command to the 8275. Since the internal counters are not running, the HRTC and VRTC signals will not be generated until another command is received by the 8275.

The Preset command might be useful for system debugging operations and could also be used to synchronize multiple 8275s that were being used in a single system. Synchronization between two or more 8275s would involve more than simply issuing the Preset command, however; some external circuitry would be required.

The 8275 Read Light Pen Register Command

The format for the Read Light Pen Register command is shown in Figure 3-14. The command byte (60_{16}) causes the 8275 to access its two internal light pen registers. The contents of these two registers are then made available on the two ensuing read operations which are performed by the microprocessor. The first byte read from the 8275 after the command is issued will be the character position on a row, and the second byte read will be the row number where the Light Pen input (LPEN) was detected. As we have mentioned previously, external delays in the light pen circuitry will cause the character count read from the Light Pen register to be displaced by three

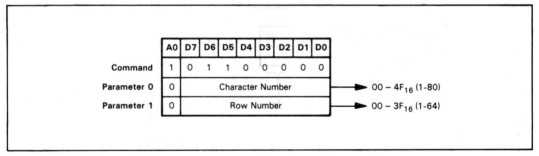

Figure 3-14. 8275 CRT Controller Read Light Pen Command

characters or more from the actual physical position where the light pen was detected. Your software must therefore adjust its value accordingly. You should also be aware that the values held in the light pen registers are not changed by reading them with the Read Light Pen Register command. Only another negative-to-positive transition of the LPEN input will cause the contents of these registers to be changed.

The 8275 Load Cursor Register Command

Figure 3-15 shows the format for the Load Cursor Register command. After the command byte (80_{16}) has been written to the 8275, the microprocessor must write two additional bytes to the 8275 to load the cursor position registers. The first byte specifies the character position (1-80) within a row where the cursor is to be displayed, while the second byte specifies the character row (1-64) for the cursor. The type of cursor symbol that will be displayed at the specified location is determined by the Reset command.

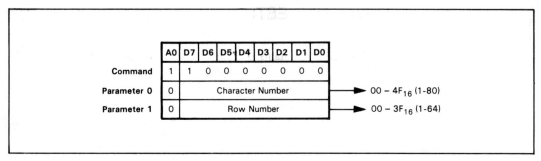

Figure 3-15. 8275 CRT Controller Load Cursor Register Command

The 8275 Enable/Disable Interrupt Commands

These two commands simply set or reset the Interrupt Enable Status bit in the 8275 Status register, and enable and disable the INT output of the 8275. If the Interrupt Enable bit is reset, then no interrupt will be generated at the end of the display of one frame of data. Note that interrupts are also enabled or disabled by the Start and Stop Display commands. The Enable Interrupt command is $A0_{16}$, while the Disable Interrupt command is $C0_{16}$.

DATA SHEETS

This section contains specific electrical and timing data for the 8275.

8275

ABSOLUTE MAXIMUM RATINGS*

Ambient Temperature Under Bias. . . . . 0°C to 70°C
Storage Temperature . . . . -65°C to +150°C
Voltage On Any Pin
    With Respect to Ground . . . . -0.5V to +7V
Power Dissipation . . . . 1 Watt

COMMENT: Stresses above those listed under "Absolute Maximum Ratings" may cause permanent damage to the device. This is a stress rating only and functional operation of the device at these or any other conditions above those indicated in the operational sections of this specification is not implied.

D.C. CHARACTERISTICS

$T_A = 0°C$ to $70°C$; $V_{CC} = 5V \pm 5\%$

SYMBOL	PARAMETER	MIN.	MAX.	UNITS	TEST CONDITIONS
V_{IL}	Input Low Voltage	-0.5	0.8	V	
V_{IH}	Input High Voltage	2.0	$V_{CC}+0.5V$	V	
V_{OL}	Output Low Voltage		0.45	V	$I_{OL} = 2.2\,mA$
V_{OH}	Output High Voltage	2.4		V	$I_{OH} = -400\,\mu A$
I_{IL}	Input Load Current		± 10	μA	$V_{IN} = V_{CC}$ to 0V
I_{OFL}	Output Float Leakage		± 10	μA	$V_{OUT} = V_{CC}$ to 0V
I_{CC}	V_{CC} Supply Current		160	mA	

CAPACITANCE

$T_A = 25°C$; $V_{CC} = GND = 0V$

SYMBOL	PARAMETER	MIN.	MAX.	UNITS	TEST CONDITIONS
C_{IN}	Input Capacitance		10	pF	$f_c = 1\,MHz$
$C_{I/O}$	I/O Capacitance		20	pF	Unmeasured pins returned to V_{SS}.

Data sheets on pages 3-40 through 3-44 are reprinted by permission of Intel Corporation.

8275

Other Timing:

SYMBOL	PARAMETER	MIN.	MAX.	UNITS	TEST CONDITIONS
t_{CC}	Character Code Output Delay		150	ns	$C_L = 50$ pF
t_{HR}	Horizontal Retrace Output Delay		150	ns	$C_L = 50$ pF
t_{LC}	Line Count Output Delay		250	ns	$C_L = 50$ pF
t_{AT}	Control/Attribute Output Delay		250	ns	$C_L = 50$ pF
t_{VR}	Vertical Retrace Output Delay		250	ns	$C_L = 50$ pF
t_{IR}	IRQ↑ from CCLK↓		250	ns	$C_L = 50$ pF
t_{RI}	IRQ↓ from Rd↑		250	ns	$C_L = 50$ pF
t_{KQ}	DRQ↑ from CCLK↓		250	ns	$C_L = 50$ pF
t_{WQ}	DRQ↑ from WR↑		250	ns	$C_L = 50$ pF
t_{RQ}	DRQ↓ from WR↓		200	ns	$C_L = 50$ pF
t_{LR}	DACK↓ to WR↓	0		ns	
t_{RL}	WR↑ to DACK↑	0		ns	
t_{PR}	LPEN Rise		50	ns	
t_{PH}	LPEN Hold	100		ns	

Note: Timing measurements are made at the following reference voltages: Output "1" = 2.0V, "0" = 0.8V.

WAVEFORMS

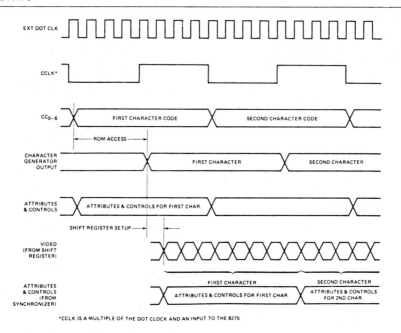

*CCLK IS A MULTIPLE OF THE DOT CLOCK AND AN INPUT TO THE 8275.

Typical Dot Level Timing

8275

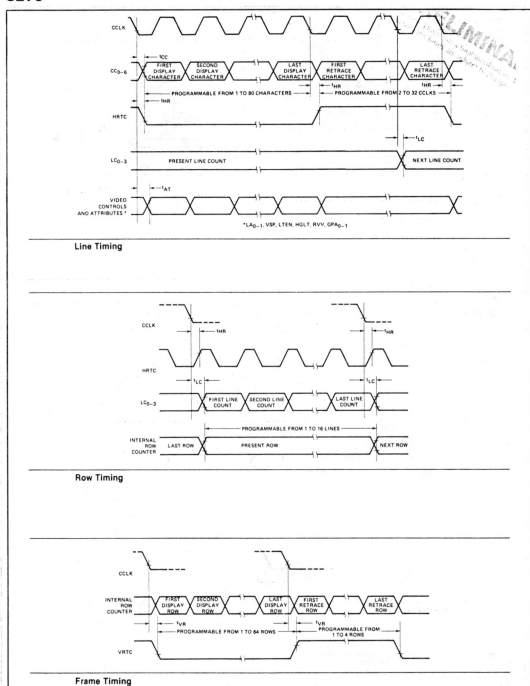

Line Timing

Row Timing

Frame Timing

8275

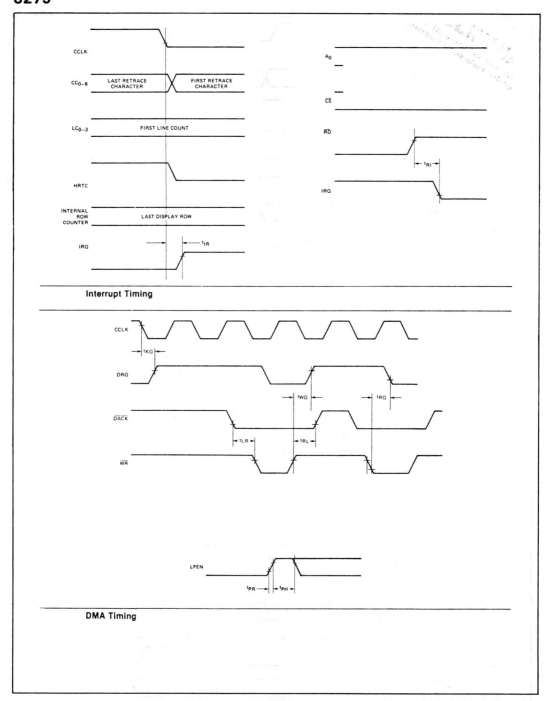

Interrupt Timing

DMA Timing

8275

A.C. CHARACTERISTICS

T_A = 0°C to 70°C; V_{CC} = 5.0V ±5%; GND = 0V

Bus Parameters (Note 1)

Read Cycle:

SYMBOL	PARAMETER	MIN.	MAX.	UNITS	TEST CONDITIONS
t_{AR}	Address Stable Before READ	0		ns	
t_{RA}	Address Hold Time for READ	0		ns	
t_{RR}	READ Pulse Width	250		ns	
t_{RD}	Data Delay from READ		200	ns	C_L = 150 pF
t_{DF}	READ to Data Floating	20	100	ns	

Write Cycle:

SYMBOL	PARAMETER	MIN.	MAX.	UNITS	TEST CONDITIONS
t_{AW}	Address Stable Before WRITE	0		ns	
t_{WA}	Address Hold Time for WRITE	0		ns	
t_{WW}	WRITE Pulse Width	250		ns	
t_{DW}	Data Setup Time for WRITE	150		ns	
t_{WD}	Data Hold Time for WRITE	0		ns	

Clock Timing:

SYMBOL	PARAMETER	MIN.	MAX.	UNITS	TEST CONDITIONS
t_{CLK}	Clock Period	320		ns	
t_{KH}	Clock High	120		ns	
t_{KL}	Clock Low	120		ns	
t_{KR}	Clock Rise	5	30	ns	
t_{KF}	Clock Fall	5	30	ns	

Note 1: AC timings measured at V_{OH} = 2.0, V_{OL} = 0.8

Write Timing

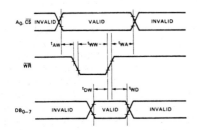

Read Timing

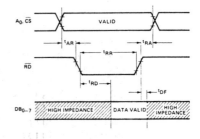

Clock Timing

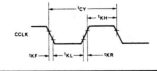

Input Waveforms (For A.C. Tests)

4

The 6845 CRT Controller

The 6845 CRT controller lies somewhere between the DP8350 device, described in Chapter 2, and the 8275 device, described in Chapter 3, in its functional organization and capabilities. It is similar to the DP8350 in the way that it is positioned functionally within a system; it coordinates the flow of data from screen memory to character generator logic and thence onto the CRT monitor, but data does not actually pass through the 6845 as is the case with the 8275 device. However, the 6845 is a fully programmable device, like the 8275, instead of being mask-programmable like the DP8350.

Figure 4-1 illustrates those logic functions of the idealized CRT controller described in Chapter 1 that are provided by the 6845. The 6845 provides screen memory addressing logic but no memory contention logic. The light pen logic, cursor logic, and scan line counters provided by the 6845 are similar to those of the 8275, although the scrolling and cursor logic is more limited in the 6845. Similarly, the blanking logic provided by the 6845 is minimal, although adequate, and does not provide as many options as the 8275. No dot timing logic is provided on-chip, as will be true with most of the CRT controllers we will describe, but the HSYNC/VSYNC generation logic is present on the 6845. We have shown the programmable registers, status, and control logic only partially shaded in Figure 4-1; while the 6845 provides a full complement of programmable registers, there are no status or control registers or signals provided by the 6845 to simplify the microprocessor interface.

The sole manufacturer of the 6845 device is:

MOTOROLA INCORPORATED
Semiconductor Products Division
3501 Ed Bluestein Boulevard
Austin, TX   78721

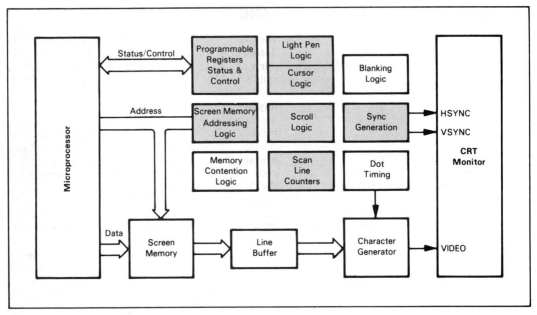

Figure 4-1. Logic Functions Provided by 6845 CRT Controller

THE 6845 CRT CONTROLLER PINS AND SIGNALS

Figure 4-2 shows the pin assignments and signals for the 6845. We will provide a brief description of each signal, since this will serve as a good introduction to, and overview of, the capabilities of the 6845. We will discuss the uses of these signals and their interrelationships in more detail later in this chapter.

The 6845 signals may be divided into three categories: signals used to interface the controller to the microprocessor and system busses, signals used to interface the controller to screen memory and character generator logic, and signals directly related to the controller-CRT monitor interface.

The microprocessor system interface signals are described below.

Microprocessor Interface Signals

D0-D7 are the bidirectional data lines used to transfer data between the microprocessor and the 6845's internal registers.

$\overline{CS}$ is a standard Chip Select input signal which would typically be generated by system address decoding logic. $\overline{CS}$ must be low to read information from or write information into one of the internal registers of the 6845.

RS is the Register Select input to the 6845. The 6845 has 19 internal registers. Rather than sacrifice five of the 40 available pins to register addressing, the 6845 uses one of its registers as an address register to access the remaining 18 registers. When the RS signal is low, the internal address register is accessed and can be loaded with the address of the internal register that is to be accessed next. When RS is high, this enables access to the register whose address is contained in the address register.

R/$\overline{W}$ is the Read/Write signal which determines whether data is to be written into a 6845 register or read out of one of the registers. R/$\overline{W}$ must be low for a write operation and high for a read operation.

E is the synchronizing clock or Enable signal required by the 6845. This signal is used to enable the internal I/O buffers and to clock data into and out of the internal registers via the data buffers. In a 6800-based system the Enable (E) input would be connected to the system's $\Phi2$ signal.

CLK is the Clock input used to synchronize all of the 6845's control signals. It will usually be derived from external dot clock logic and is usually the character rate clock, at least in an alphanumeric application. Thus it is actually more closely associated with the character generator and video interface, but we have included it with the microprocessor system interface signals since it is the primary timing input to the 6845.

$\overline{RESET}$ is a standard device Reset signal which initializes the 6845. When $\overline{RESET}$ goes low, all of the internal counters are cleared and all of the 6845's output signals are set low. The video display operation of the 6845 is thus effectively stopped. The reset operation does not affect the program-accessible counters within the 6845, however, so that display can be resumed when the $\overline{RESET}$ signal returns high.

V_{CC} (+ 5 V) and V_{SS} (ground) are standard power supply connections to the 6845.

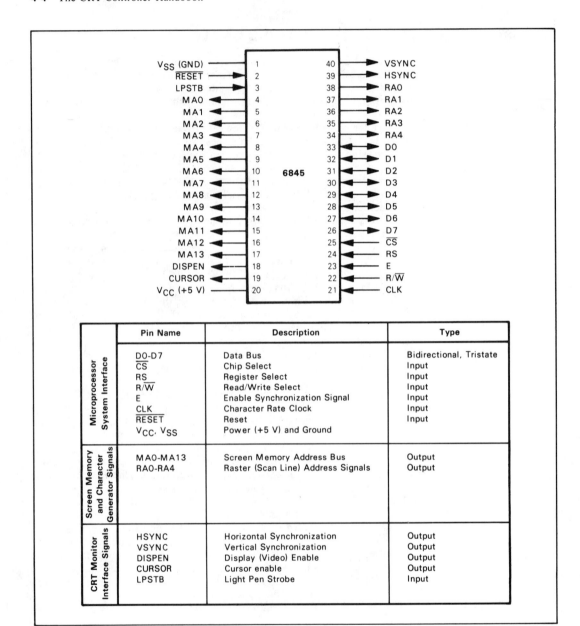

Figure 4-2. 6845 CRT Controller Pins and Signals

Screen Memory and Character Generator Signals   There are two sets of signals provided by the 6845 to implement the interface to screen memory and character generator logic: MA0-MA13 are the screen Memory Address outputs and RA0-RA4 are the Raster Address output signals to character generator logic. The 14 screen Memory Address outputs (MA0-MA13) allow the 6845 to access up to 16K bytes of screen memory. The Raster Address output lines (RA0-RA4) are the outputs from the 6845's scan line counter. While the signal names used on the 6845 for these outputs differ from those which we have used elsewhere in this book, these five signals are simply the scan line counts required by character generator logic to determine which scan line of a character row is being displayed.

CRT Monitor Signals   The 6845 provides a fairly standard set of CRT monitor interface signals. HSYNC and VSYNC are the standard Horizontal and Vertical Synchronization signals required by CRT monitors. DISPEN is the Display Enable signal and will be set high whenever the video signal to the CRT monitor is to be active. DISPEN will be set low during horizontal and vertical retrace, and thus might also be called the video blanking signal. CURSOR is the standard cursor enable signal used to create a steady stream of dots on a CRT screen to produce a cursor symbol.

LPSTB is the Light Pen Strobe input signal which, in conjunction with external circuitry, can be used to implement a light pen interface between the CRT monitor and the 6845. When the 6845 detects a high level on the LPSTB signal it saves the contents of the screen memory address counter in one of the internal register sets so that the microprocessor can subsequently determine the position at which the light pen was detected.

THE 6845 CRT CONTROLLER PROGRAMMABLE REGISTERS

The 6845 provides 19 internal registers which must be accessed under program control to establish operating parameters for the device. Figure 4-3 illustrates the logic involved in accessing the registers. Accessing one of the 18 parameter registers requires a two-step sequence: first, the 5-bit Address register must be loaded with the number of the operating parameter that is to be accessed, and you can then perform a read or write of the addressed register. The Register Select (RS) signal determines whether it is the Address register that is being accessed or one of the parameter registers. Transfers of address and parameter information to and from the registers occurs via the data lines (D0-D7).

Table 4-1 summarizes the function of each of the 18 parameter registers. As you can see, the first group of registers (R0 through R3) establishes the horizontal format and timing parameters, the next group (R4 through R9) determines vertical format and timing characteristics, and the remaining registers (R10 through R17) deal with cursor characteristics, screen memory addressing, and the light pen interface. Typically, registers R0 through R11 will be loaded when the system is first started up and will not have to be accessed thereafter. The remaining six registers (R12 through R17) will be accessed on an ongoing basis during system operation. R12 and R13 establish a 14-bit starting (or top of page) address for screen memory. The contents of these registers can be manipulated to perform scrolling of the screen contents. Registers 14 and 15 establish a 14-bit cursor address to produce the cursor symbol on the screen. Registers 16 and 17 will be used if the light pen input is utilized.

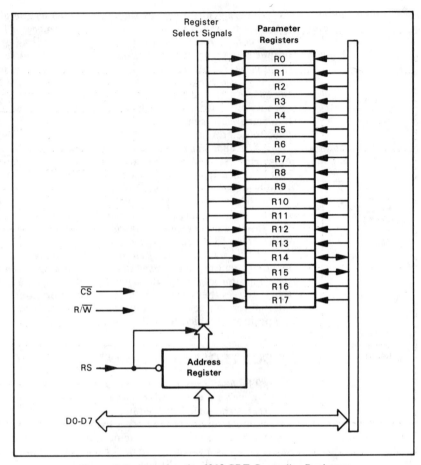

Figure 4-3. Accessing the 6845 CRT Controller Registers

Typically, **the 6845 will occupy two memory or I/O addresses; the RS signal would be connected to the system's least significant address bit (A0).** When A0 is low, the Address register would be accessed to load it with the number of the desired parameter register. That specified register would then be accessed by setting A0 high. **Thus a typical register access operation would consist of two consecutive device write cycles, or a write cycle followed by a read cycle, and these cycles would be directed to consecutive memory or I/O locations.** Since the contents of the parameter registers determine all of the primary operating characteristics for the 6845, we shall defer a description of the contents of each register until later in this chapter when we describe programming of the device.

Table 4-1. 6845 CRT Controller Programmable Registers

	Register		Read (R) Write (W)	Bits	Range — Units
	No.	Name/Function			
Horizontal Format and Timing	0 (00$_{16}$)	Horizontal Total	W	8	1 – 256 (0-FF$_{16}$) CLKs
	1 (01$_{16}$)	Characters/Row	W	8	1 – 256 (0-FF$_{16}$) CLKs
	2 (02$_{16}$)	HSYNC Position	W	8	1 – 256 (0-FF$_{16}$) CLKs
	3 (03$_{16}$)	HSYNC Width	W	4	1 – 16 (0-F$_{16}$) CLKs
Vertical Format and Timing	4 (04$_{16}$)	Vertical Total	W	7	1–128 (0-7F$_{16}$) Character Rows
	5 (05$_{16}$)	VSYNC Adjust	W	5	1 – 32 (0-1F$_{16}$) Scan Lines
	6 (06$_{16}$)	Character Rows/Frame	W	7	1–128 (0-7F$_{16}$) Character Rows
	7 (07$_{16}$)	VSYNC Position	W	7	1–128 (0-7F$_{16}$) Character Rows
	8 (08$_{16}$)	Interlace Mode	W	2	0-3
	9 (09$_{16}$)	Scan Lines/Row	W	5	1 – 32 (0-1F$_{16}$) Scan Lines
Primary Operating Registers	10 (0A$_{16}$)	Cursor Start Scan Line	W	7*	1 – 32 (0-1F$_{16}$) Scan Lines
	11 (0B$_{16}$)	Cursor Stop Scan Line	W	5	1 – 32 (0-1F$_{16}$) CLKs
	12 (0C$_{16}$)	(MSB) Start Address (Top of Page)	W	6	1 – 16,384 (0000-4FFF$_{16}$)
	13 (0D$_{16}$)	(LSB)	W	8	
	14 (0E$_{16}$)	(MSB) Cursor Position	R/W	6	0 – 16,384 (0000-4FFF$_{16}$)
	15 (0F$_{16}$)	(LSB)	R/W	8	
	16 (10$_{16}$)	(MSB) Light Pen Position	R	6	0 – 16,384 (0000-4FFF$_{16}$)
	17 (11$_{16}$)	(LSB)	R	8	

* Two bits used to specify cursor blink characteristics

THE 6845-MICROPROCESSOR SYSTEM INTERFACE

Since the 6845 is a member of the 6800 family of devices, the interface that it provides to the microprocessor system is a standard 6800-type interface. The signals used to interface the controller to the microprocessor consist of the eight data lines (D0-D7), the Chip Select ($\overline{\text{CS}}$) signal, the Register Select (RS) signal, the Read/Write (R/$\overline{\text{W}}$) signal, and the Enable (E) signal.

The microprocessor can transfer parameter information to and from the 6845 simply by issuing standard memory write and read commands to the device (recall that the 6800 family uses memory-mapped I/O). **Timing for a microprocessor-initiated write operation to load an address into the Address register or a parameter into one of the parameter registers can be illustrated as follows:**

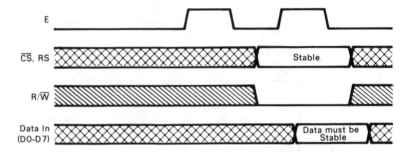

This timing is completely straightforward with the exception of the E signal. In a 6800 system, this signal would be driven by the Φ2 clock. This is a continuous clock signal in 6800 systems and is used to trigger all data transfer between the system microprocessor and its supporting devices. **In a system that uses a CPU other than a 6800 family device or 6502 microprocessor, you must derive and supply some type of continuous clock signal to drive the E input to the 6845.** Since there is a maximum allowable cycle time for the E input signal, it is necessary that it be driven by a continuous clock. This may result in a rather complicated interface to the microprocessor in a non-6800 system.

The timing for a microprocessor-initiated read operation to obtain information from the parameter registers of the 6845 can be illustrated as follows:

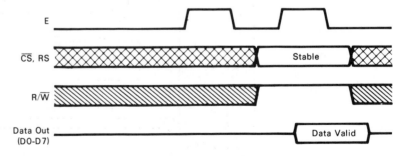

Once again, with the exception of the E signal, this timing is completely straightforward.

The read and write cycles we have just illustrated are the only communication that occurs directly between the microprocessor system and the 6845. Unlike some of the other CRT controllers we have described, the 6845 provides no interrupt signals, DMA or memory contention signals, or status signals. In addition, the 6845 does not include a data register (data for display goes directly from screen memory to character generator logic), a status register, or a command register. The bulk of microprocessor interaction with the 6845 will be during system startup when the parameter register must be loaded with values to establish timing characteristics.

THE 6845-SCREEN MEMORY/CHARACTER GENERATOR INTERFACE

The only signals that the 6845 device provides specifically for the screen memory interface are the 14 memory address outputs (MA0-MA13). At the beginning of a frame, the 6845's internal address counter is set to the value contained in the Start Address (or Top of Page) register (R12, R13). Thereafter, the contents of the 6845's address counter, and thus of the memory address outputs, are incremented at the Character Clock (CLK) rate during each scan line. At the end of each scan line, the address register will once again be set to the start address and the cycle repeated until all scan lines comprising a character row have been completed. Upon completion of one character row, the address counter will be loaded with the address of the first character on the next character row.

Screen memory address timing is quite straightforward and similar to that which we have described, and will describe, for other CRT controllers in this book. **The one aspect of the screen memory interface which this timing does not deal with is memory contention resolution** to determine when the microprocessor system can access screen memory without disrupting the accesses initiated by the 6845. **To see what might be required, we need to examine the position of the 6845 within the system. The following illustration shows the general relationship between the 6845, microprocessor, screen memory, and character generator logic.**

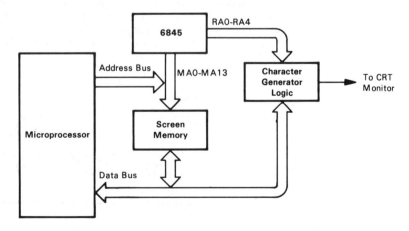

Data will be loaded into screen memory under control of the microprocessor and will then be accessed by the 6845 to cause the contents of screen memory to be presented to character generator logic. This arrangement is similar to that which we encountered with the DP8350 in Chapter 2. Screen memory data does not pass through the 6845, as was the case with the 8275 device described in Chapter 3. Neither is the 6845 involved in initiating the DMA transfers of data within the system.

There are numerous methods which can be used to resolve memory contention. You can use external logic to decode the scan lines (as indicated by RA0-RA4) to determine when the 6845 will not need access to screen memory, and then allow the microprocessor access to the busses during these intervals. You can also use the horizontal blanking and vertical blanking intervals to grant access to the microprocessor. These techniques are familiar ones which we discussed in Chapter 1 and have seen with the CRT controllers described in Chapters 2 and 3. **The point we should make here is that the 6845 provides no logic specifically to assist you in implementing this external circuitry to resolve memory contention.**

Interleaved Access to Screen Memory

There is one characteristic of the 6845, or more accurately of the 6800-type systems, **that can be used to implement interleaved access to screen memory. In a 6800-based system,** a two-phase clock is used to time all transactions in the system; the CPU will utilize system busses only during one of these phases. In such a system, **you can use $\Phi2$ as the Enable (E) input to the 6845. The 6845 can then utilize the system busses to access screen memory during the alternate phases** and there will be no interference between the 6845 and the microprocessor. **The timing for this arrangement can be illustrated as follows:**

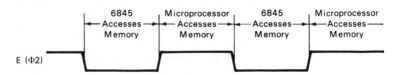

The interface that the 6845 provides to character generator logic simply consists of the five Raster Address or scan line counter outputs (RA0-RA4). These outputs form one set of inputs to character generator logic, while the data from screen memory comprises the second set of character code inputs to character generator logic.

The RA0-RA4 outputs can represent scan line counts ranging from 0 to 31, and thus character rows can be comprised of up to 32 scan lines. **Register R9 specifies the number of scan lines per character row,** and thus the maximum count that RA0-RA4 will reach before being reset to 0. **The scan line counter will be incremented at the Horizontal Synchronization (HSYNC) rate. Timing for the RA0-RA4 outputs can be illustrated as follows:**

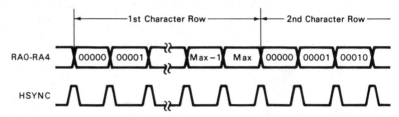

The timing illustrated here is for a standard non-interlaced display. The 6845, however, can also operate in two interlaced modes of operation, and the scan line counter function is somewhat dependent on the mode you specify. Therefore, let us now discuss the various interlaced and non-interlaced modes provided by the 6845.

The 6845 CRT Controller Scan Modes

The 6845 provides three scan modes: standard non-interlaced scans, interlaced-sync scanning, and interlaced-sync-and-video scanning. You select the desired mode by loading the appropriate 2-bit code into Register R8, the Interlace Mode register. These bits specify the mode as shown below:

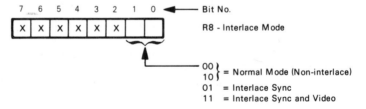

Non-Interlaced Mode

Creation of a character in the standard, non-interlaced mode can be illustrated as follows:

Scan Line Number	RA4-RA0
0	00000
1	00001
2	00010
3	00011
4	00100
5	00101
6	00110
7	00111
8	01000

In this mode, every horizontal scan line is traced during each vertical scan, and the refresh rate for each dot on the screen is thus the VSYNC frequency (for example, 60 Hz). This non-interlaced mode is the most commonly used in alphanumeric terminals and is the only mode provided by most of the CRT controllers we describe.

**Interlaced-
Sync Mode**
In the interlaced-sync mode, the first sweep (the even field) starts at the upper left-hand corner of the screen and the second sweep (odd field) starts at the top center of the screen. (For an illustration of interlaced fields refer to Chapter 1.) In the interlaced-sync mode, the same information is presented on the screen in both the odd and even fields. This can be illustrated as follows:

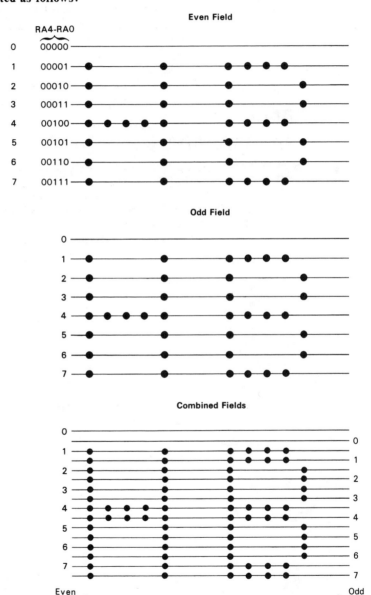

Interlaced-Sync Mode Timing

The same information is repeated in the even and odd fields and the two fields are displaced vertically from one another by one-half scan line. Thus the combined fields improve resolution by making the letters appear to have nearly solid vertical lines due to the proximity of the adjacent dots. **A problem with this approach is that each field is refreshed at one-half of the VSYNC rate (for example, 30 Hz). This may result in an unacceptable flicker of the dots on the screen.** As we discussed in Chapter 1, flicker due to low refresh rate can be overcome by using long-persistence phosphor CRT screens.

The timing for the interlaced-sync mode can be illustrated as follows:

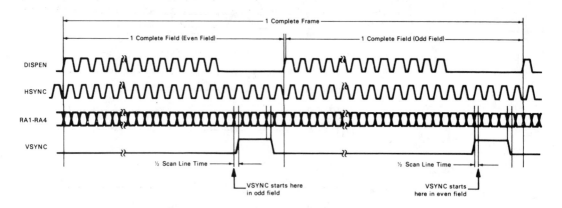

All scan line counts for every character row will be generated during both the odd and even fields so that the same dot patterns from the character generator will be output twice — once during each field. The VSYNC pulse for the odd field occurs one-half scan line time earlier during the odd field than it does during the even field; this is what produces the one-half scan line vertical separation between scan lines of the odd and even fields.

Interlaced-Sync with-Video Mode

In the interlaced-sync-with-video mode, dot information is also written into both the odd and even fields of a frame. In this case, however, the same information is not presented in both fields; instead, half of each character is written in each field so that a character row comprised of eight scan lines will have four scan lines presented in the even field and four in the odd field. This can be illustrated as follows:

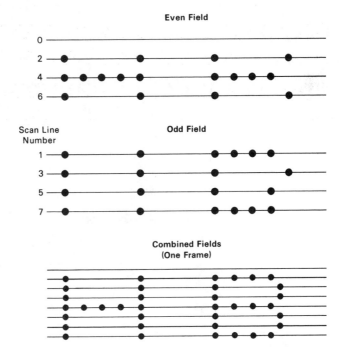

**Interlaced-Sync-
with-Video
Mode Timing**

This mode of operation results in the highest screen density, since each character row is only half as tall as in the other two modes we illustrated. This mode suffers from the same weakness as the interlaced-sync mode, however, in that each dot will only be refreshed at one-half the VSYNC frequency. The low refresh rate may be even more objectionable in this mode than in the interlaced-sync mode, since only half the character is being created in each field.

The timing for this interlaced-sync-and-video mode can be illustrated as follows:

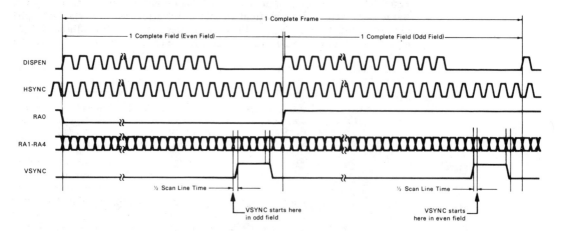

Since only odd-numbered scan lines are produced during the odd field in this mode, RA0 is always high during the odd field. During the even field, RA0 will be held low so that the dot patterns sent to character generator logic will only be those for even-numbered scan lines.

THE 6845-CRT MONITOR INTERFACE

Figure 4-4 illustrates the signals provided by the 6845 to implement the interface to a CRT monitor. The 6845 provides fewer signals and options than did the 8275 device described in Chapter 3, but gives you more options than were provided by the DP8350 described in Chapter 2.

The Horizontal Synchronization (HSYNC) and Vertical Synchronization (VSYNC) signals are the standard signals compatible with three-terminal CRT monitors. You specify the exact time at which these pulses are to be generated by loading the appropriate values into the parameter registers. The duration of the HSYNC pulse is also program-specifed. The VSYNC pulse, however, is of a fixed duration (16 scan line times) and thus external logic may be required to obtain a pulse of the proper duration for a given CRT monitor. The HSYNC and VSYNC signals can, of course, be combined using external components to produce a composite SYNC signal or composite video signal for those CRT monitors requiring this type of input.

The CURSOR signal is generated by the 6845 whenever the screen memory address is equal to the address contained in the 6845's Cursor Position register (R14, R15). This signal is similar to that provided by the DP8350 and 8275 devices. Since there is no symbol for the cursor stored in screen memory, the CURSOR signal must be used by external logic to generate a continuous stream of dots to create the cursor symbol on the screen. As we shall see when we discuss programming of the 6845's registers, you have the option of specifying that a blinking cursor symbol be generated. The 6845 will accomplish this blinking by not turning on the CURSOR signal on at the specified character position during some of the refresh operations. This approach is more straightforward than that used by the 8275, which manipulated yet another signal (video suppression) to produce a blinking cursor.

The DISPEN signal will be set high during horizontal and vertical retrace operations and thus can be used as the blanking signal to turn off VIDEO during these intervals. You specify those points when the DISPEN signal is to be activated by loading the appropriate values into the parameter registers. Those intervals where DISPEN is to be activated have no fixed relationship to the occurrence of the HSYNC or VSYNC signals. Instead, the DISPEN signal will be activated at all times except during those intervals where you have specified that characters are to be displayed on the screen.

Both the CURSOR and DISPEN signals are synchronized to the screen memory address outputs; that is, when the screen memory address corresponding to the cursor position, or the position where the display is to be blanked, is generated, the CURSOR or DISPEN signal will be activated at that time. However, since some time will be required to access the corresponding character from screen memory and then to generate the dot pattern via character generator logic and shift it out through the video shift register, the CURSOR and DISPEN signals may be activated far before the corresponding character is being sent to the screen. Therefore, you may have to introduce delays using the appropriate logic for both signals to account for this pipelining effect.

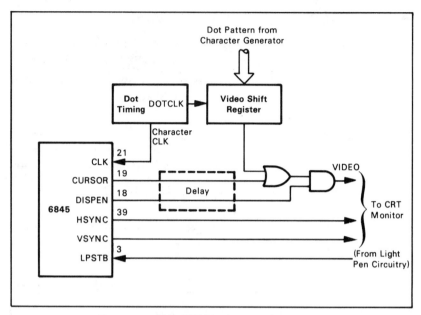

Figure 4-4. 6845 CRT Monitor Interface Signals

The **LPSTB (Light Pen Strobe) input to the 6845 requires a negative-to-positive transition from external circuitry to cause the controller to store its current screen memory address value in the internal Light Pen registers (R16, R17).** Storage of the screen memory address is synchronized with the Character Clock (CLK) input to the 6845 as shown in the following illustration:

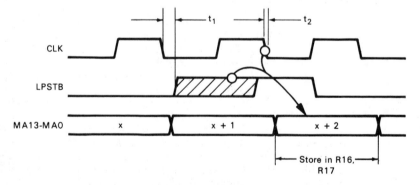

After LPSTB has gone high, the next positive-to-negative transition of CLK causes the subsequently generated screen memory address to be saved in the Light Pen registers. Since there may be significant delays introduced by the external light pen circuitry, you may have to adjust the values held on the light pen registers using software in order to obtain a true screen position value. In addition, **there are two critical timing relationships in the preceding illustration: if LPSTB goes high during t_1 or t_2, the 6845 may store a screen memory**

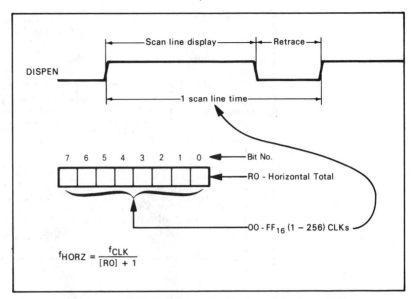

Figure 4-5. 6845 CRT Controller Horizontal Registers (R0)

address other than the X + 2 address illustrated. Therefore you must use external circuitry to synchronize the presentation of LPSTB with the CLK signal to ensure that it is presented to the 6845 at the proper time. For exact timing specifications, refer to the 6845 data sheets at the end of this chapter.

PROGRAMMING THE 6845 CRT CONTROLLER REGISTERS

The 18 parameter registers provided by the 6845 can be divided into three groups: those used to establish horizontal format and timing, those used to establish vertical format and timing, and those used to establish cursor shape and location, screen memory addressing, and light pen address information. All of the registers, with the exception of the Cursor Position and Light Pen Position registers, are write-only registers. As we have discussed previously, accessing any of these registers is a two-step process; you must first load the address register with the 5-bit address which selects the parameter register that is subsequently to be accessed.

Horizontal Format and Timing Registers

Registers R0 through R3 establish horizontal format and timing for the 6845. These registers are usually loaded with the required values at system startup and do not have to be changed thereafter.

Figure 4-5 shows the format for the Horizontal Total register (R0). The contents of this register determine the total time allotted for one scan line in terms of Character Clock (CLK) cycles. This register contains the total of displayed and undisplayed characters, minus 1, per horizontal line, thus determining the HSYNC frequency.

**Figure 4-6 shows the format for the Character/Row register (R1).
This register specifies the number of characters to be displayed on each
horizontal line.** Once again this register is loaded with the total number of
characters minus 1, and the units for this register are Character Clocks
(CLKs).

**Figure 4-7 shows the format for the HSYNC Position register (R2).
This register establishes the point where the HSYNC signal makes its negative-to-positive transition** and is specified in terms of Character Clocks
(CLKs). The reference point for the beginning of the HSYNC pulse is the left-
most character position displayed on the scan line.

**Figure 4-8 shows the format for the HSYNC Width register (R3).
Only the four least significant bits of this register are used,** and they establish the duration of the HSYNC pulse in the range of 1 to 16 Character Clocks
(CLKs). This allows you to adjust the HSYNC pulse duration to meet the
requirements of specific CRT monitors.

**The following illustration shows the relationships between the four
horizontal timing and format registers (R0-R3) in terms of t_{CLK}:**

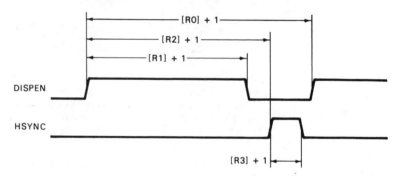

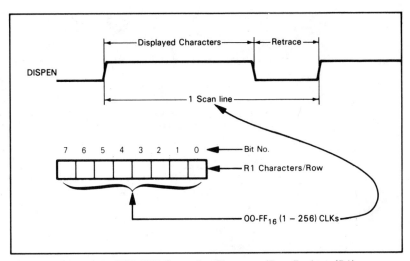

Figure 4-6. 6845 CRT Controller Characters/Row Register (R1)

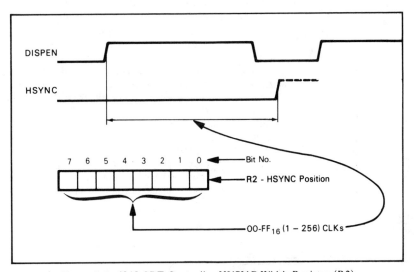

Figure 4-7. 6845 CRT Controller HYSNC Width Register (R2)

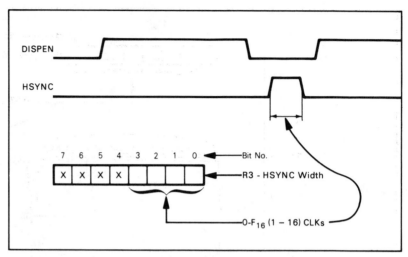

Figure 4-8. 6845 CRT Controller YSYNC Width Register (R3)

Vertical Format and Timing Registers The next six registers (R4-R9) establish the vertical format and timing. Just as was the case with the horizontal parameter registers, these registers will usually be loaded with the desired values at system startup and will not have to be changed thereafter. The point of reference for all of the vertical timing and parameter registers is the topmost character position displayed on the screen.

Figure 4-9 shows the format for the Vertical Total register (R4) and the VSYNC Adjust register (R5). These registers determine the total number of scan line times in a frame, including the time required for vertical retrace, and thus specify the overall frame rate or VSYNC frequency. The Vertical Total register (R4) is a 7-bit register, and the units used are character rows. Since a character row can consist of up to 32 scan lines, this specification may be too gross to allow you to establish a refresh frequency close to the line frequency (for example, 60 Hz). Thus you can use the VSYNC Adjust register (R5) to fine tune the VSYNC frequency. The VSYNC Adjust register is a 5-bit register, and the units used are scan line times.

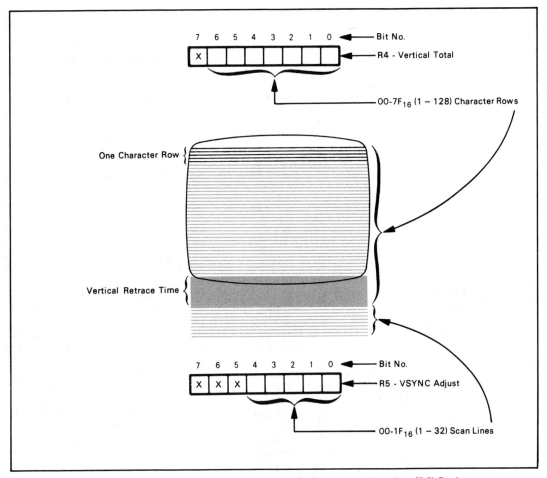

Figure 4-9. 6845 CRT Controller Vertical Total (R4) and VYSNC Adjust (R5) Registers

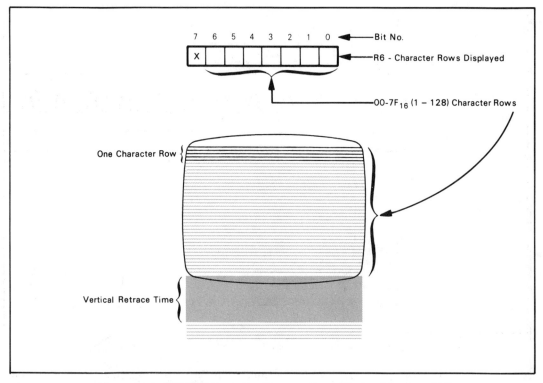

Figure 4-10. 6845 CRT Controller Character Rows Displayed Register (R6)

Figure 4-10 shows the format for the Character Rows Displayed register (R6). This 7-bit register allows you to specify that up to 128 character rows be displayed. Note that this specification does not determine the position of the VSYNC pulse, but instead determines that point when the Display Enable (DISPEN) signal will be set low for the vertical retrace operation.

Figure 4-11 shows the format for the VSYNC Position register (R7). This 7-bit register determines the point where the VSYNC signal makes its negative-to-positive transition to initiate vertical retrace. The VSYNC position is specified by means of the character row times measured from the beginning of the first character row on the screen. You can see in Figure 4-11 that the VSYNC pulse always has a duration of 16 scan line times. Since the scan line frequency will vary from application to application, and since you cannot adjust the VSYNC pulse duration, you may need external circuitry in order to achieve a VSYNC pulse that is compatible with the CRT monitor you are using.

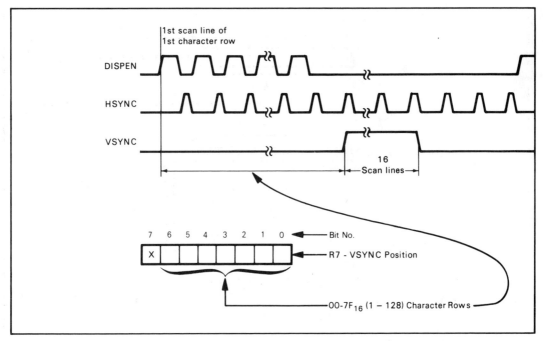

Figure 4-11. 6845 CRT Controller VYSNC Position Register (R7)

Register R8 is the Interlace Mode register which determines whether an interlaced or non-interlaced scan will be used. To see the format fr this register, refer to the section earlier in this chapter where the interlaced scan modes were discussed in detail.

Figure 4-12 shows the format for Register R9, which determines the number of scan lines per character row. This is a 5-bit register, and you can thus specify that a character row be comprised of up to 32 scan lines. The value you specify in this register determines the maximum count that will be output on the Raster (scan line) Address signals (RA0-RA4) which are sent to the character generator logic. You load R9 with the desired scan line count minus 1.

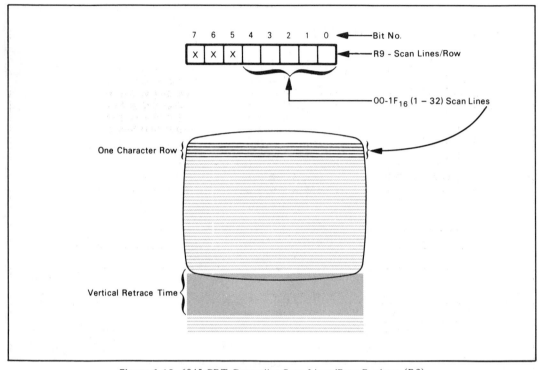

Figure 4-12. 6845 CRT Controller Scan Lines/Row Register (R9)

The next two registers in the 6845 determine the type of cursor that is to be displayed. Figure 4-13 shows the format for the Cursor Start register (R10) and the Cursor Stop register (R11). The five least significant bits of each register determine the scan lines within a character row where the CURSOR signal is to be activated. The scan line specified in Register R10 is the first scan line where the CURSOR signal is to be set high, and CURSOR will be set high for all subsequent scan lines in that character position until the scan line specified in Register R11 has been completed. Thus **if you want the cursor symbol to occupy a single scan line, you must load the same value into both Registers R10 and R11. A block cursor symbol will be produced if R10 and R11 contain different values.** If you have specified that the 6845 is to operate in the interlaced-sync-and-video mode, then the Cursor Start and Stop registers must both be loaded with even or odd values. To see why this is so, refer to our earlier discussion of the interlaced modes of operation.

Bits 5 and 6 of the Cursor Start register determine whether a blinking cursor is to be displayed. You can specify that the Cursor signal be blinked at 1/16 or 1/32 of the field rate.

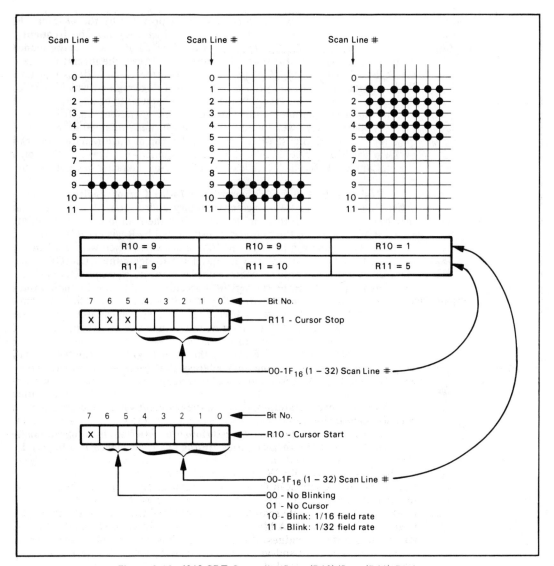

Figure 4-13. 6845 CRT Controller Start (R10)/Stop (R11) Registers

Primary
Operating
Registers

The remaining six registers (R12-R17) provided by the 6845 can be considered the primary operating registers, since they may be frequently accessed and manipulated during operation instead of simply being loaded with values at system startup time. Figure 4-14 shows the format for these six registers. The six registers are arranged as three 14-bit address registers. Registers R12 and R13 comprise a 14-bit Top of Page register which specifies the screen memory address containing the first character to be displayed on the screen. Upon completion of the vertical retrace operation, the first screen memory address that is generated will be that which is contained in the Top of Page register. By changing the contents of the Top of Page register, you can perform scrolling. Since the 6845 addresses memory linearly rather than on a row/column basis, scrolling can be on a character-by-character basis or row-by-row.

Registers R14 and R15 comprise a 14-bit Cursor Position register. When the 6845 generates a screen memory address on MA0-MA13 that matches the contents of this register, and when the scan line counter outputs (RA0-RA4) fall within the boundaries established by Registers R10 and R11, the CURSOR signal will be activated. As we discussed when we described the interface to the CRT monitor, you may have to delay the CURSOR signal using external logic in order to achieve display at the desired character position. Movement of the cursor on the screen is accomplished by loading new values into the Cursor Position register. Registers R14 and R15 are the only ones provided by the 6845 that are read/write registers, so you can use this register pair to keep track of where the cursor is, rather than having to copy the cursor position to it from another memory location.

Registers R16 and R17 comprise the 14-bit Light Pen register and will be loaded with the screen memory address that corresponds to the screen position where the LPSTB signal was detected. You should refer to our earlier discussion of the LPSTB signal since there are several critical timing parameters involved with this signal and the resultant values that are stored in the Light Pen register.

Figure 4-15 illustrates the relationship between the programmable registers of the 6845 and a modified timing chain developed in Chapter 1.

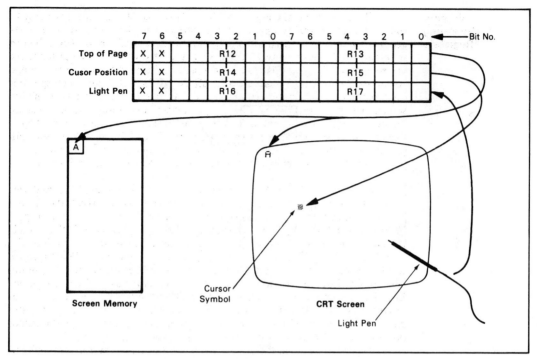

Figure 4-14. 6845 CRT Controller Operating Registers (R12-R17)

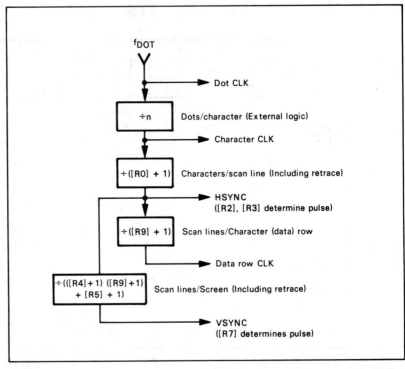

Figure 4-15. The Relationship between 6845 Programmable Registers and the CRT Timing Chain

DATA SHEETS

This section contains specific electrical and timing data for the 6845.

6845

SYSTEM BLOCK DIAGRAM DESCRIPTION

As shown in Figure 1, the primary function of the CRTC is to generate refresh addresses (MA0-MA13), row selects (RA0-RA4), and video monitor timing (HSYNC, VSYNC) and Display Enable. Other functions include an internal cursor register which generates a Cursor output when its contents compare to the current Refresh Address. A light-pen strobe input signal allows capture of Refresh Address in an internal light pen register.

All timing in the CRTC is derived from the Clk input. In alphanumeric terminals, this signal is the character rate. Character rate is divided down from video rate by external High Speed Timing when the video frequency is greater than 3 MHz. Shift Register, Latch, and MUX Control signals are also provided by external High Speed Timing.

The processor communicates with the CRTC through a buffered 8-bit Data Bus by reading/writing into the 18-register file of the CRTC.

The Refresh Memory address is multiplexed between the Processor and CRTC. Data appears on a Secondary Bus which is buffered from the processor Primary Bus. A number of approaches are possible for solving contentions for the Refresh Memory.

1. Processor always gets priority.
2. Processor gets priority access anytime, but can be synchronized by an interrupt to perform accesses only during horizontal and vertical retrace times.
3. Synchronize processor by memory wait cycles.
4. Synchronize processor to character rate (See Figure 2). The 6800 MPU family lends itself to this configuration because it has constant cycle lengths. This method provides zero burden on the processor because there is never a contention for memory. All accesses are *"transparent."*

The secondary data bus concept in no way precludes using the Refresh RAM for other purposes. It looks like any other RAM to the Processor. For example, using Approach 4, a 64K byte RAM Refresh Memory could perform refresh and program storage functions transparently.

MAXIMUM RATINGS

Rating	Symbol	Value	Unit
Supply Voltage	V_{CC}*	-0.3 to +7.0	Vdc
Input Voltage	V_{in}*	-0.3 to +7.0	Vdc
Operating Temperature Range	T_A	0 to +70	°C
Storage Temperature Range	T_{stg}	-55 to +150	°C

*With respect to V_{SS} (Gnd).

RECOMMENDED OPERATING CONDITIONS

Characteristics	Symbol	Min	Typ	Max	Unit
Supply Voltage	V_{CC}	4.75	5.0	5.25	Vdc
Input Low Voltage	V_{IL}	-0.3	—	0.8	Vdc
Input High Voltage	V_{IH}	2.0	—	V_{CC}	Vdc

FIGURE 2 — TRANSPARENT REFRESH MEMORY CONFIGURATION TIMING USING 6800 MPU FAMILY

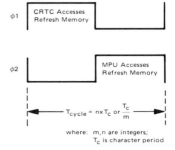

$$T_{cycle} = n \times T_c \text{ or } \frac{T_c}{m}$$

where: m,n are integers;
T_c is character period

6845

ELECTRICAL CHARACTERISTICS (V_{CC} = 5.0 V ±5%, V_{SS} = 0, T_A = 0 to 70°C unless otherwise noted)

Characteristic		Symbol	Min	Typ	Max	Unit
Input High Voltage		V_{IH}	2.0	–	V_{CC}	Vdc
Input Low Voltage		V_{IL}	-0.3	–	0.8	Vdc
Input Leakage Current		I_{in}	–	1.0	2.5	µAdc
Three-State (V_{CC} = 5.25 V) (V_{in} = 0.4 to 2.4 V)		I_{TSI}	-10	2.0	10	µAdc
Output High Voltage (I_{load} = -205 µA) (I_{load} = -100 µA)	D0-D7 Other Outputs	V_{OH}	2.4 2.4	– –	– –	Vdc
Output Low Voltage (I_{load} = 1.6 mA)		V_{OL}	–	–	0.4	Vdc
Power Dissipation		P_D	–	600	–	mW
Input Capacitance	D0-D7 All others	C_{in}	– –	– –	12.5 10	pF
Output Capacitance	All Outputs	C_{out}	–	–	10	pF
Minimum Clock Pulse Width, Low		PW_{CL}	160	–	–	ns
Minimum Clock Pulse Width, High		PW_{CH}	200	–	–	ns
Clock Frequency		f_c	–	–	2.5	MHz
Rise and Fall Time for Clock Input		t_{cr}, t_{cf}	–	–	20	ns
Memory Address Delay Time		t_{MAD}	–	–	160	ns
Raster Address Delay Time		t_{RAD}	–	–	160	ns
Display Timing Delay Time		t_{DTD}	–	–	300	ns
Horizontal Sync Delay Time		t_{HSD}	–	–	300	ns
Vertical Sync Delay Time		t_{VSD}	–	–	300	ns
Cursor Display Timing Delay Time		t_{CDD}	–	–	300	ns
Light Pen Strobe Minimum Pulse Width		PW_{LPH}	100	–	–	ns
Light Pen Strobe Disable Time		t_{LPD1}	–	–	120	ns
		t_{LPD2}	–	–	0	ns

Note: The light pen strobe must fall to low level before VSYNC pulse rises.

BUS TIMING CHARACTERISTICS

Characteristic	Symbol	Min	Max	Unit
READ/WRITE				
Enable Cycle Time	t_{cycE}	1.0	–	µs
Enable Pulse Width, High	PW_{EH}	0.45	25	µs
Enable Pulse Width, Low	PW_{EL}	0.43	–	µs
Setup Time, $\overline{CS}$ and RS valid to enable positive transition	t_{AS}	160	–	ns
Data Delay Time	t_{DDR}	–	320	ns
Data Hold Time (Read) (write)	t_H	10 10	– –	ns
Address Hold Time	t_{AH}	10	–	ns
Rise and Fall Time for Enable Input	t_{Er}, t_{Ef}	–	25	ns
Data Setup Time	t_{DSW}	195	–	ns
Data Access Time	t_{ACC}	–	480	ns

6845

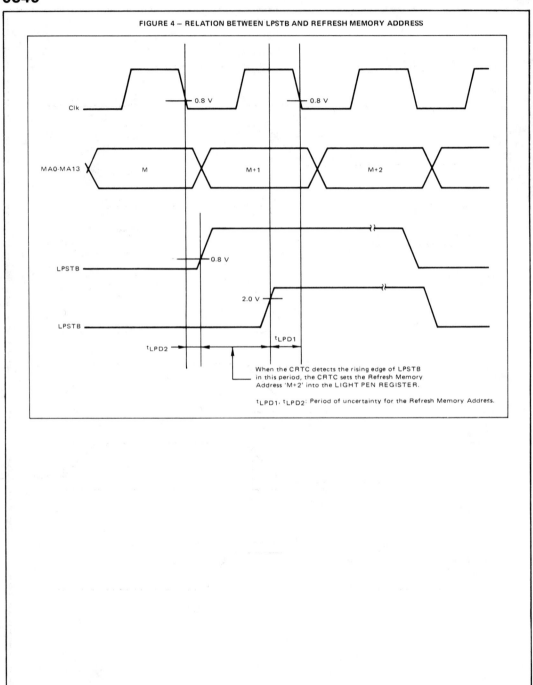

FIGURE 4 – RELATION BETWEEN LPSTB AND REFRESH MEMORY ADDRESS

When the CRTC detects the rising edge of LPSTB in this period, the CRTC sets the Refresh Memory Address 'M+2' into the LIGHT PEN REGISTER.

t_{LPD1}, t_{LPD2}: Period of uncertainty for the Refresh Memory Address.

6845

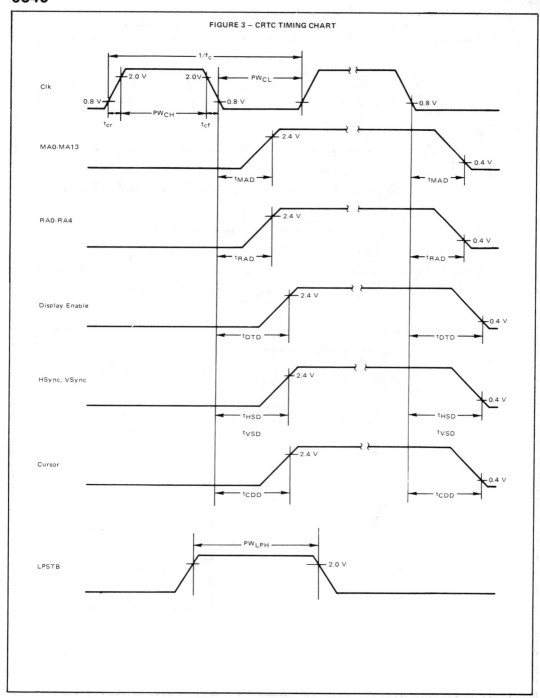

FIGURE 3 – CRTC TIMING CHART

6845

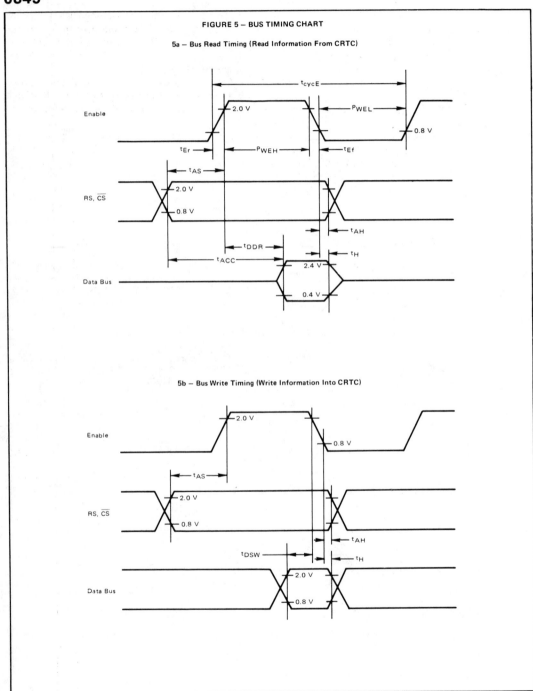

FIGURE 5 — BUS TIMING CHART

5a — Bus Read Timing (Read Information From CRTC)

5b — Bus Write Timing (Write Information Into CRTC)

6845

FIGURE 6 – BUS TIMING TEST LOAD

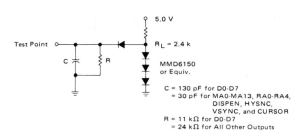

FIGURE 7 – PIN ASSIGNMENT

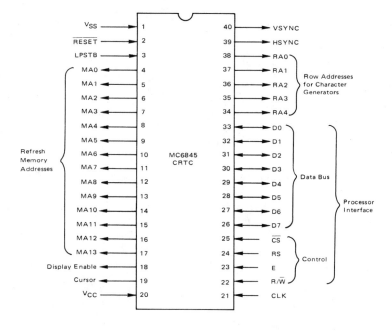

6845

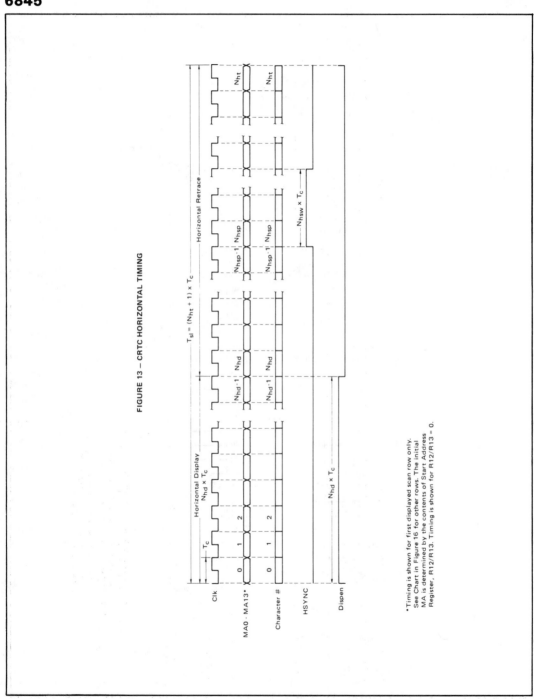

FIGURE 13 – CRTC HORIZONTAL TIMING

*Timing is shown for first displayed scan row only. See Chart in Figure 16 for other rows. The initial MA is determined by the contents of Start Address Register, R12/R13. Timing is shown for R12/R13 = 0.

6845

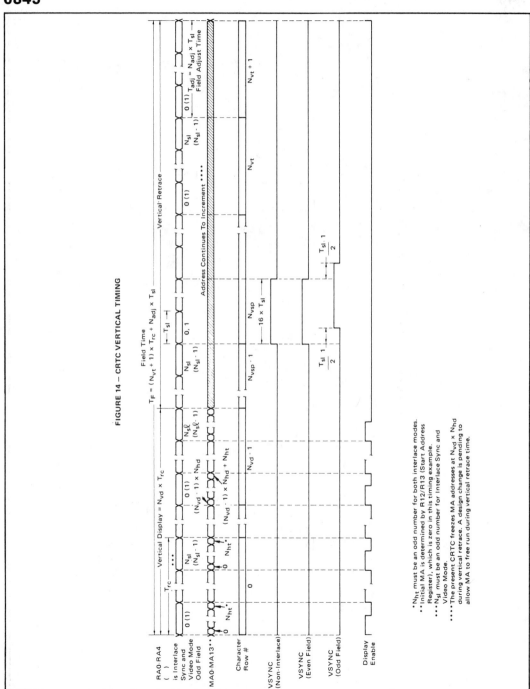

FIGURE 14 — CRTC VERTICAL TIMING

* N_{ht} must be an odd number for both interlace modes.
** Initial MA is determined by R12/R13 (Start Address Register), which is zero in this timing example.
*** N_{sl} must be an odd number for Interlace Sync and Video Mode.
**** The present CRTC freezes MA addresses at $N_{vd} \times N_{hd}$ during vertical retrace. A design change is pending to allow MA to free run during vertical retrace time.

6845

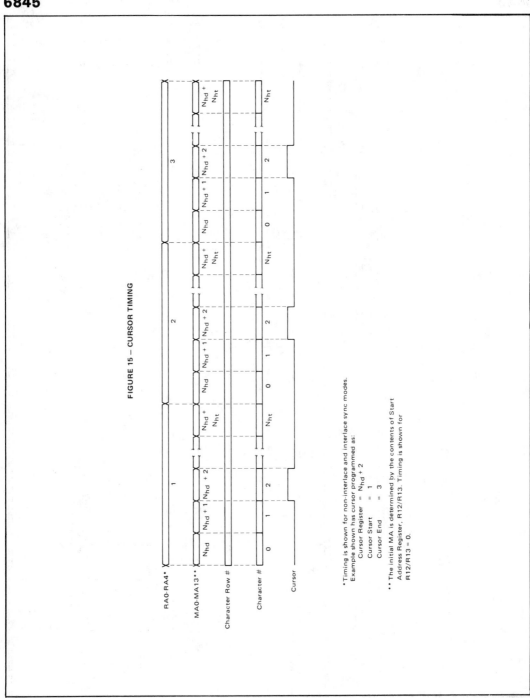

FIGURE 15 – CURSOR TIMING

6845

FIGURE 16 – REFRESH MEMORY ADDRESSING (MA0-MA13) STATE CHART

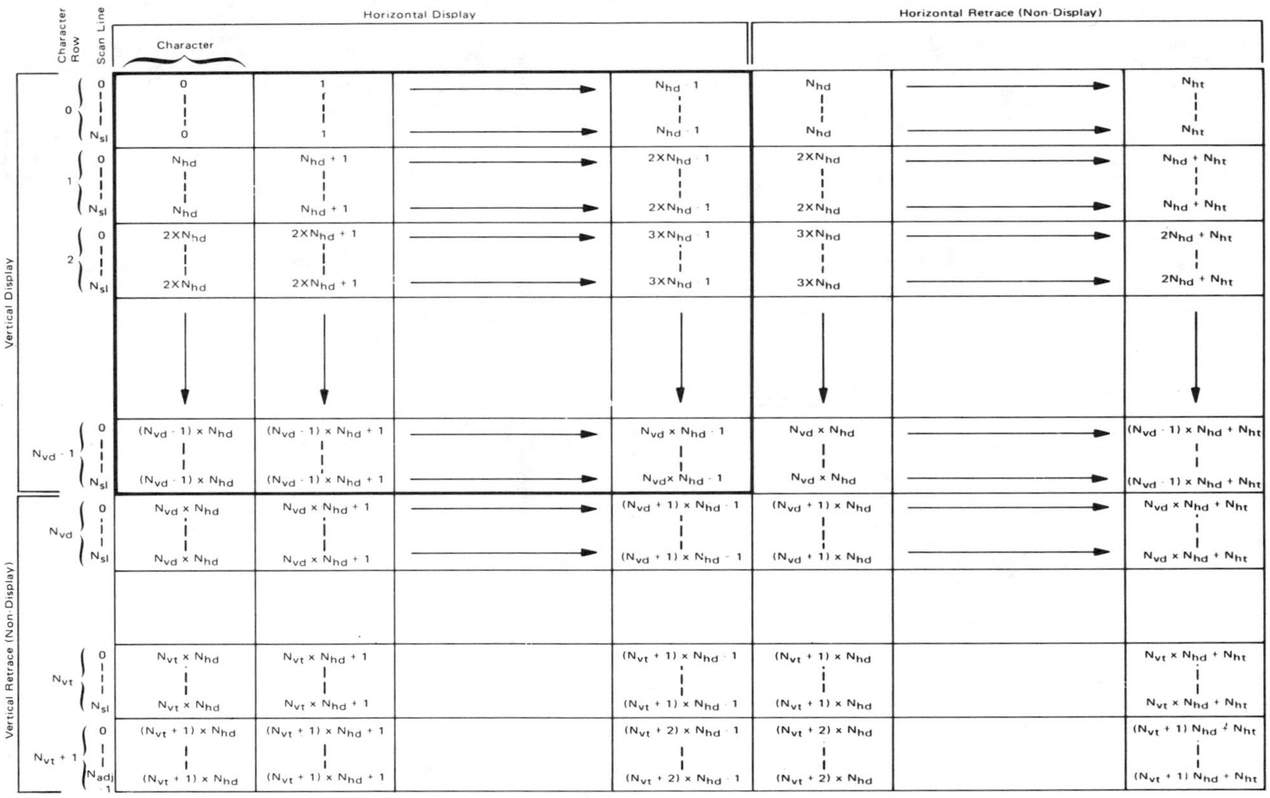

NOTE 1 The initial MA is determined by the contents of start address register, R12/R13. Timing is shown for R12/R13 = 0. Only Non Interlace and Interlace Sync Modes are shown.

NOTE 2 The present CRTC freezes MA addresses at $N_{vd} \times N_{hd}$ during vertical retrace. A design change is pending to allow MA to free run during vertical retrace time.

5

The 6545 CRT Controller

The 6545 CRT controller is the 6500-equivalent of the 6845 device which we described in Chapter 4. The two devices are pin-compatible and functionally equivalent, except that a few additional functions have been added to the 6545. Because the differences are few, we will not provide a complete description of the 6545 CRT controller; instead, we will discuss only those aspects of the 6545 device that are different from the 6845 CRT controller.

Figure 5-1 illustrates those logic functions of the idealized CRT controller, described in Chapter 1, that are provided by the 6545 device. If you compare this figure to the equivalent one for the 6845 device (Figure 4-1), you will see that the only differences are that the blocks labeled **Programmable Registers, Status,** and **Control** are completely shaded for the 6545 rather than partially shaded, and that the memory contention logic which was not present on the 6845 is provided on the 6545. While most of the programmable registers provided by the 6545 are identical to those of the 6845, the 6545 device also provides a Status register which can be read by the microprocessor to ascertain the progress of operations within the device. The 6845 provided no such status register. Because of its presence on the 6545 device, we have shown the logic block in Figure 5-1 as being fully present. A more significant difference is in the memory contention logic function. The 6845 provided absolutely no logic specifically to simplify memory contention within the system. The 6545 device, on the other hand, provides some rather unusual logic that can be used to resolve memory contention between the CRT controller and the microprocessor.

There are two sources for the 6545 CRT controller:

SYNERTEK, INC.	ROCKWELL INTERNATIONAL
1901 Old Middlefield Way	Microelectronic Devices
Mountain View	P.O. Box 3669, RC55
CA 94043	Anaheim, CA 92803

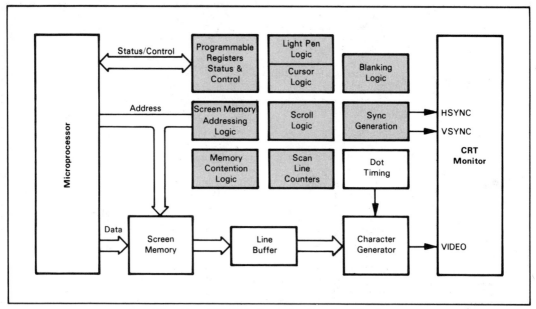

Figure 5-1. 6545 CRT Controller Functional Logic

THE 6545 CRT CONTROLLER PINS AND SIGNALS

Figure 5-2 shows the pin and signal assignments for the 6545 CRT controller. Only those signals which are shaded in the figure are different from those of the 6845, and they are the only ones we will discuss here.

The Φ2 signal is the system clock input to the 6545 and was named the Enable (E) signal on the 6845 device. This signal is used to trigger all data transfers between the microprocessor and the 6545, thus **performing the same function as the E signal on the 6845. There is one potentially significant difference, however:** the 6845's E signal had a maximum cycle time specified and thus had to be driven by a continuous clock signal. The Φ2 **signal on the 6545,** on the other hand, **has no maximum limit for cycle time** and thus need not be driven by a continuous clock. This will simplify the microprocessor interface to the 6545 in non-6500-compatible systems.

The screen Memory Address outputs (MA0-MA13) have a second set of signal names associated with them. The eight least significant address signals are labeled CC0-CC7 and can function as Character Column address outputs, while the six most significant signals can serve as Character Row address outputs (CR0-CR6). You have the option of specifying that the 6545 address screen memory in the straight binary sequence, using MA0-MA13, or in a row/column addressing sequence using CC0-CC7/CR0- CR5.

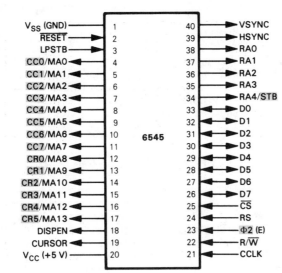

☐ These signals differ from 6845 signals

	Pin Name	Description	Type
Microprocessor System Interface	D0-D7	Data Bus	Bidirectional, Tristate
	$\overline{CS}$	Chip Select	Input
	RS	Register Select	Input
	R/$\overline{W}$	Read/Write Select	Input
	Φ2 (E)	System Synchronization Signal	Input
	CCLK	Character Rate Clock	Input
	$\overline{RESET}$	Reset	Input
	V_{CC}, V_{SS}	Power (+5 V) and Ground	
Screen Memory and Character Generator Signals	MA0-MA13	Screen Memory Address Bus (Linear)	Output
	(CC0-CC7, CR0-CR5)	Screen Memory Column/Row Addresses	Output
	RA0-RA3	Raster (Scan Line) Address Signals	Output
	RA4/STB	Raster Address/Update Address Strobe	Output
CRT Monitor Interface Signals	HSYNC	Horizontal Synchronization	Output
	VSYNC	Vertical Synchronization	Output
	DISPEN	Display (Video) Enable	Output
	CURSOR	Cursor Enable	Output
	LPSTB	Light Pen Strobe	Input

Figure 5-2. 6545 CRT Controller Pins and Signals

The most significant Raster Address output (RA4) has also been assigned a secondary signal name: Strobe (STB). This signal is associated with the memory contention logic provided by the 6545. If you program the 6545 to operate in a transparent memory adressing mode, the STB signal can be used to inform external logic of those intervals when a memory update address (as opposed to a memory display address) is being output on the MA0-MA13 lines. We will discuss the STB signal in more detail when we describe the screen memory interface provided by the 6545 device. You should note that if the transparent memory addressing option is utilized, external logic must be supplied if you need to use this signal as RA4. We will describe the required logic later in this chapter.

THE 6545 CRT CONTROLLER PROGRAMMABLE REGISTERS

The programmable registers provided by the 6545 are, for the most part, identical to those of the 6845; there are, however, a few minor changes and several significant additions. Figure 5-3 illustrates the logic involved in accessing the programmable registers of the 6545, and Table 5-1 summarizes the function of each of the programmable registers. In both Figure 5-3 and Table 5-1, those areas that are shaded are the only ones that differ from the corresponding functions of the 6845 and will be the only functions which we will discuss here.

The programmable registers of the 6545 are accessed in the same way as in the 6845: you first load the Address register with a 5-bit address which subsequently is used to specify the Parameter register that is to be accessed. The following table shows how the Chip Select ($\overline{CS}$), Register Select (RS), and Read/Write (R/$\overline{W}$) signals are used to select the various registers:

$\overline{CS}$	RS	R/$\overline{W}$	Function
H	X	X	Device not selected
L	L	L	Write data into Address Register
L	L	H	Read data from Status Register
L	H	L	Write data into register specified by Address Register
L	H	H	Read data from register specified by Address Register

Status Register

This logic is the same as with the 6845 with the exception of the Status register; the 6845 provided no status register. The 6545 Status register can be accessed by the microprocessor at any time and provides three bits of information. The bit assignments for the Status register are shown in Figure 5-4. The five least significant bits are not used and will also be zero when you read the contents of the Status register.

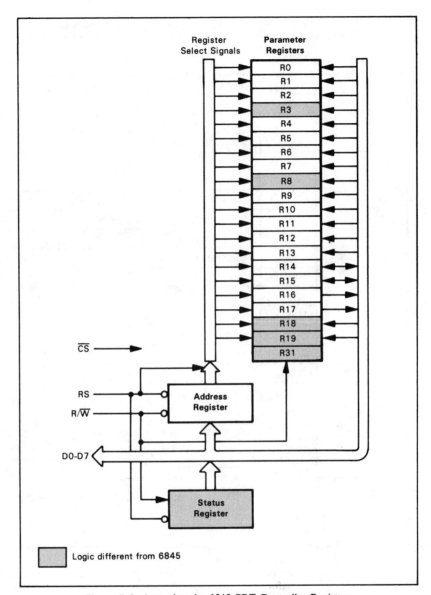

Figure 5-3. Accessing the 6545 CRT Controller Registers

Table 5-1. 6545 CRT Controller Programmable Registers

	Register		Read (R) Write (W)	Bits	Range — Units
	No.	Name/Function			
Horizontal Format and Timing	0 (00₁₆)	Horizontal Total	W	8	1 – 256 (0-FF₁₆) CCLKs
	1 (01₁₆)	Characters/Row	W	8	1 – 256 (0-FF₁₆) CCLKs
	2 (02₁₆)	HSYNC Position	W	8	1 – 256 (0-FF₁₆) CCLKs
	3 (03₁₆)	HSYNC/VSYNC Width	W	4 + 4	1 – 16 (0-F₁₆) CCLKs
Vertical Format and Timing	4 (04₁₆)	Vertical Total	W	7	1–128 (0-7F₁₆) Character Rows
	5 (05₁₆)	VSYNC Adjust	W	5	1 – 32 (0-1F₁₆) Scan Lines
	6 (06₁₆)	Character Rows/Frame	W	7	1–128 (0-7F₁₆) Character Rows
	7 (07₁₆)	VSYNC Position	W	7	1–128 (0-7F₁₆) Character Rows
	8 (08₁₆)	Mode Control	W	8	See Figure 5-7
	9 (09₁₆)	Scan Lines/Row	W	5	1 – 32 (0-1F₁₆) Scan Lines
Primary Operating Registers	10 (0A₁₆)	Cursor Start Scan Line	W	7*	1 – 32 (0-1F₁₆) Scan Lines
	11 (0B₁₆)	Cursor Stop Scan Line	W	5	1 – 32 (0-1F₁₆) CCLKs
	12 (0C₁₆)	(MSB) Start Address (Top of Page)	W	6	1 – 16,384 (0000-4FFF₁₆)
	13 (0D₁₆)	(LSB)	W	8	
	14 (0E₁₆)	(MSB) Cursor Position	R/W	6	0 – 16,384 (0000-4FFF₁₆)
	15 (0F₁₆)	(LSB)	R/W	8	
	16 (10₁₆)	(MSB) Light Pen Position	R	6	0 – 16,384 (0000-4FFF₁₆)
	17 (11₁₆)	(LSB)	R	8	
	18 (12₁₆)	(MSB) Update Location	W	6	0 – 16,384 (0000-4FFF₁₆)
	19 (13₁₆)	(LSB)	W	8	
	31 (1F₁₆)	Increment Update		-	N/A

* Two bits used to specify cursor blink characteristics

▨ Functions different from 6845

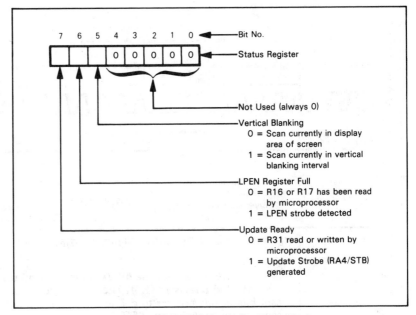

Figure 5-4. 6545 CRT Controller Status Register

Bit 5 of the Status register is the Vertical Blanking status bit and will be set to 1 during vertical retrace operations while vertical blanking takes place. The timing for this bit is illustrated in Figure 5-5. This bit can be checked by the microprocessor to determine when it can access screen memory without disturbing the contents of the screen, since the 6545 does not require access to screen memory while the vertical blanking bit is set. To reduce the possibility of timing conflicts near the end of the vertical blanking interval, bit 5 will be reset five CCLK periods before the end of the vertical blanking interval, so that microprocessor access to screen memory can be terminated before the 6545 begins to access screen memory for the first scan line on the screen.

Bit 6 of the Status register is the LPEN Register full bit. Whenever a negative-to-positive transition on the LPEN input to the 6545 is detected, this bit will be set to 1 and will remain set until you read the contents of the Light Pen Position register (R16 or R17). The presence of this bit corrects a logic deficiency of the 6845, since there was no way, with that device, of determining when a new value had been stored in the Light Pen Position register.

Bit 7 of the Status register is the Update Ready bit. If you have specified operation in the transparent screen memory addressing mode, this bit will be set whenever an update strobe is sent out on the RA4/STB pin. The bit will be reset when you access the Update Increment (R31) register. We shall defer further discussion of bit 7 and its use until we discuss the screen memory interface in detail.

If you refer once again to Figure 5-3 and Table 5-1, you will see that five of the Parameter registers are shown shaded. Two of these registers (R3 and R8) have enhanced functions beyond their equivalent registers in a 6545, while the last 3 registers (R18, R19, and R31) are new registers beyond those provided by the 6845.

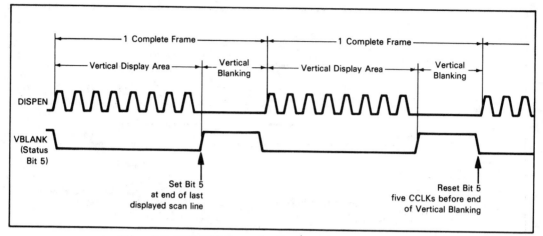

Figure **5-5**. 6545 CRT Controller Vertical Blanking Status Timing

Figure 5-6 shows the bit assignments and functions of the HSYNC/ VSYNC Width register (R3). The 6845 device used only the four least significant bits of this register to define the HSYNC duration. This function is the same on **the 6545,** but the 6545 device also **uses the four most significant bits to define a pulse duration for the VSYNC pulse.** You can specify that VSYNC be from 1 to 16 scan lines in duration, which may eliminate the need for external logic to interface the 6545 to a CRT monitor.

Figure 5-7 shows the bit assignments for the Mode Control register (R8). In the 6845 device, only the 2 least significant bits of this register were used, and they specified the interface mode that the device was to operate in. These two bits serve the same function in the 6545 controller and you should refer to Chapter 4 for a description of the interlace modes of operation available.

Bit 2 of the Mode Control register specifies the screen memory addressing mode that is to be used. If this bit is set to 0, the MA0-MA13 outputs will generate straight binary addresses for screen memory. If bit 2 is set to a 1, row/column addressing will be used and the screen memory address outputs will be generated on a Character Column (CC0-CC7) and Character Row (CR0-CR5) basis. The straight binary addressing allows more efficient use of memory while the row/column addressing is better suited for manipulation of screen data. For a discussion of the advantages and disadvantages of each method, refer to Chapter 1.

Bit 3 of the Mode Control register defines the screen memory access mode that is to be used; if this bit is 0, it specifies shared memory accessing, and if set to 1, transparent memory accessing is specified. In the shared memory access mode, the microprocessor and the 6545 utilize the same address bus to access screen memory, and external logic must be provided to resolve memory contention. This is the same approach used with the 6845 device, which provided no internal memory contention logic. The transparent memory accessing mode utilizes the logic provided by the 6545 to resolve memory contention; it results in transparent, unimpeded access to screen memory by both the microprocessor and the 6545 with minimal external logic required. We will discuss this technique in detail when we describe the interface to screen memory later in this chapter.

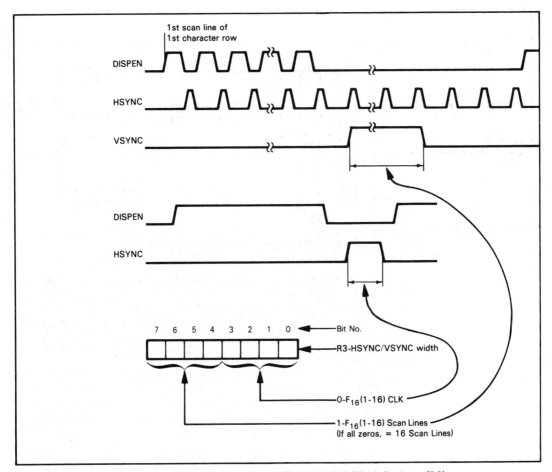

Figure 5-6. 6545 CRT Controller HYSNC/VSYNC Width Register (R3)

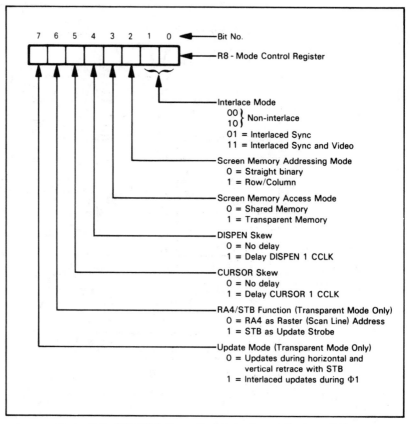

Figure 5-7. 6545 CRT Controller Mode Control Register (R8)

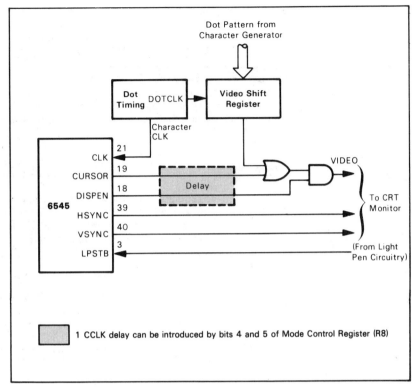

Figure 5-8. Logic Function of CURSOR/DISPEN Skew Bits in the
6545 Mode Control Register

**Bits 4 and 5 of the Mode Control register allow you to introduce a 1
CCLK delay in the generation of DISPEN and CURSOR signals** and thus
skew or displace these signals one character time to allow for delays introduced
by screen memory access and character generator logic. **Figure 5-8 shows the
interface between the 6545 device and a CRT monitor and the logic function
that can be implemented by setting bits 4 or 5 of the Mode Control register.**

Bit 6 of the Mode Control register is used if the 6545 is operating in the
transparent screen memory access mode, and **specifies whether the RA4/STB
output signal is to function as a Raster (scan line) Address output to
character generator logic or as an update Strobe (STB) signal.** Once again we
will defer a detailed discussion of the use of this bit until we describe the screen
memory interface.

Bit 7 of the Mode Control register is also associated with screen memory
logic. It **specifies the update technique that is to be used when the 6545 operates in the transparent screen memory addressing mode.** You can specify that
CPU modification of screen memory data occurs only during horizontal or vertical retrace, or that microprocessor accesses to memory be interleaved with
those of the 6545.

Registers R18 and R19 comprise the 14-bit Update register. This register can be loaded by the microprocessor with a screen memory address which can then be subsequently output by the 6545 on the MA0-MA13 lines. The register is used in the transparent memory addressing mode and is the major element in the memory contention circuitry provided by the 6545 device. We shall describe in detail how this register is used when we discuss the screen memory interface provided by the 6545. It is named the Update register since **its primary function will be to specify a screen memory location — and thus a physical screen location — that is to be updated by writing new data at that location.**

THE 6545-SCREEN MEMORY INTERFACE

There are two general types of interfaces to screen memory that can be implemented in a 6545 system: shared memory and transparent memory interfaces. In the shared memory interface, both the microprocessor and the 6545 address and access screen memory directly. This type of interface can be illustrated as follows:

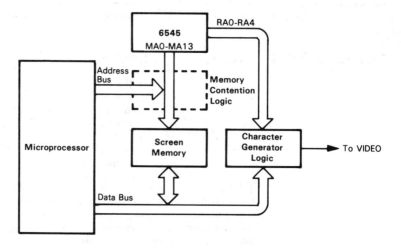

Since both the microprocessor and the 6545 must be able to address screen memory, you must supply some sort of external memory contention logic to resolve conflicts between the two. This is the same configuration described for the 6845 and many of the other CRT controllers. You should refer to our description of the 6845 screen memory interface for a discussion of how memory contention can be resolved. That discussion also applies to the 6545 although **there is one additional aid provided by the 6545; you can check the status of bit 5 of the 6545's Status register to determine when vertical retrace is being performed.** You can then grant unlimited screen memory access to the microprocessor during this vertical retrace interval. The 6845 device provided no such status bit and you therefore had to use additional external logic to determine when vertical retrace occurs.

In all other respects, the 6545 operates in the same way as the 6845 in this shared memory configuration. Let us now turn our attention to the transparent memory addressing mode available with the 6545.

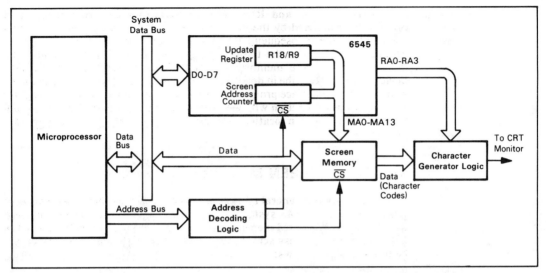

Figure 5-9. 6545 CRT Controller Transparent Memory Addressing Configuration

The 6545 CRT Controller Transparent Memory Addressing Mode

Figure 5-9 shows the general system configuration that is implied by the 6545's transparent memory addressing mode. In this mode, the microprocessor does not directly address screen memory. Instead, all screen memory addresses are generated by the 6545 and sent out on the MA0-MA13 pins. The address that is output can come from one of two sources: the 6545's internal screen address counter which is incremented at the character rate as each scan line is displayed, or from the Update register-pair (R18,R19). The Update register-pair is the means by which the microprocessor specifies screen memory locations that it needs to access. The 6545 then takes care of resolving memory contention and outputs the address from the Update register at the appropriate time. The obvious advantage of this method of addressing is that screen memory does not consume microprocessor address space.

There are two different schemes that can be used in this transparent addressing mode: the 6545 can output the address contained in the Update register-pair during $\Phi 2$ of every clock cycle, or the update address can be output during horizontal and vertical blanking intervals. You specify which of these schemes is used via bit 7 of the Mode Control register (R8). Let us first look at the $\Phi 1/\Phi 2$ interleaved scheme.

Interleaved
Transparent
Addressing

The timing for the interleaved type of transparent memory addressing can be illustrated as follows:

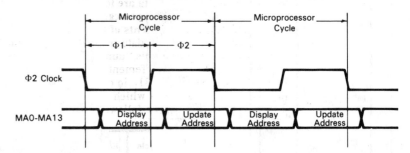

During the $\Phi1$ portion of the clock cycle, the 6545 will output the contents of its internal scan address counter to access data that is to be displayed on the screen. **During the $\Phi2$ portion, the MA0-MA13 pins from the 6545 will contain the address from the Update register.** Thus the microprocessor can indirectly access screen memory during this $\Phi2$ portion of every cycle. This technique is the same as we described in Chapter 4 for the 6845, but in this case the 6545 performs the multiplexing of the addresses and no external logic is required. **However, this scheme is not quite so straightforward as the timing diagram above implies. To see what is involved, let us examine a typical sequence that must occur for the microprocessor to write a byte of data into screen memory.**

First, the microprocesser must load the Update register-pair in the 6545 with the screen memory address where data is to be read from or written into. This process requires that you direct four successive write operations to the 6545 as listed in the following table:

I/O Cycle	R/$\overline{\text{W}}$	RS	D0-D7 Contents
1	L	L	18_{10} (R18 address)
2	L	H	Update address (MSB)
3	L	L	19_{10} (R19 address)
4	L	H	Update address (LSB)

After this 4-write cycle sequence has been completed, the 6545 will output the address that has just been loaded into the Update register during the $\Phi1$ portion of each clock cycle. Now, **to actually write a byte of data into the desired screen memory location, the microprocessor must perform one more write operation. During this write cycle, the microprocessor can treat screen memory as an I/O location.** This means that the microprocessor must generate an address which will produce a chip select signal for screen memory, supply the write signal to load the data into memory, and present the data on the data lines to memory. The 6545 will, however, generate the address signals required to specify the location within screen memory where the data is to be loaded.

**Auto-Increment
of Update
Register**

This is a rather lengthy and involved sequence simply to load one byte of data into screen memory. **The operation becomes much simpler, however, if additional bytes of data are to be written into screen memory in consecutive locations. In this case you can utilize the 6545's capability of automatically incrementing the contents of the Update register-pair.** In order to increment the contents of the Update register-pair, you must access register R31 in the 6545. Each access of this "dummy" register causes the contents of the Update register-pair to be incremented. Of course, you must first load the 6545's Address register with 31_{10} in order to select this Automatic Increment register. **Our 4-step sequence which we illustrated earlier would now consist of 5 steps as shown in the following table:**

I/O Cycle	R/$\overline{W}$	RS	D0-D7 Contents
1	L	L	12_{16} (R18 address)
2	L	H	Update address (MSB)
3	L	L	13_{16} (R19 address)
4	L	H	Update address (LSB)
5	L	L	$1F_{16}$ (R31 address)

After the five write cycles shown in the preceding illustration have been performed, the microprocessor can begin writing data to screen memory. Once again screen memory can be treated by the microprocessor as an I/O port. If the chip select signal derived from the microprocessor address bus to select memory is also used to generate the CS input to the 6545, and if RS is high, then a dummy access of R32 will be performed causing the contents of the Update register-pair to be incremented. From that point on, each write operation performed to transfer a byte of data from the microprocessor to screen memory would also select R31 in the 6545 device to increment the contents of the Update register. Thus, as long as you are loading data into consecutive screen memory locations, only one write cycle is required to perform each data transfer and the 6545 will output the appropriate update address during the Φ2 time. So, **a total of 6 write operations are required to transfer the first byte of data from the microprocessor to screen memory, but thereafter only a single write cycle is required to transfer each byte of data, as long as consecutive memory addresses are being accessed. This sequence is illustrated in the following table.**

I/O Cycle	R/$\overline{W}$	RS	D0-D7 Contents
1	L	L	12_{16} (R18 address)
2	L	H	Update address (MSB)
3	L	L	13_{16} (R19 address)
4	L	H	Update address (LSB)
5	L	L	$1F_{16}$ (R31 address)
6-n	L	H	Data to Memory and Increment R18/R19

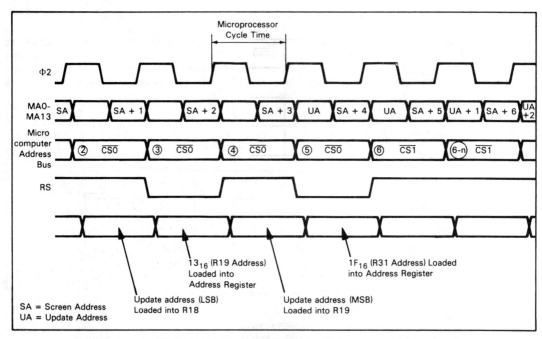

Figure 5-10. 6545 Timing Sequences for Interlaced, Transparent Addressing with Auto-Increment

The timing for this sequence is illustrated in Figure 5-10. The circled numbers ② through ⑥ , shown within the microprocessor address bus in this figure, correspond to the steps in the preceding table. You will also note in this figure that we have shown two different chip select signals ($\overline{CS0}$, $\overline{CS1}$) being output on the microprocessor address bus. When the microprocessor is writing the update data to screen memory, it must generate chip select for both screen memory and the 6545 if the automatic incrementing of the Update register is to occur. Figure 5-11 illustrates the general chip select logic demanded for this transparent addressing with auto-increment operation. The $\overline{CS0}$ signal would select the 6545 to access its Address register or one of the Parameter registers. The $\overline{CS1}$ signal generates chip select for both the 6545 and screen memory. This would be used to cause the contents of the Update register in the 6545 to be incremented as a byte of data is transferred to screen memory.

Retrace Transparent Addressing

The second method of transparent screen memory addressing available with the 6545 is to allow the microprocessor access during horizontal and vertical retrace intervals. The configuration implied in this mode of transparent memory addressing is illustrated in Figure 5-12.

There are many similarities between the interleaved transparent mode which we just described and this retrace mode. In both cases, the 6545 provides all addresses to screen memory, but here the contents of the Update register will be output to screen memory only during horizontal and vertical retrace intervals instead of being interleaved during $\Phi 1/\Phi 2$ clock periods. The contents of the Update register-pair can also be automatically incremented, as we described for the interleaved mode, by ensuring that when the

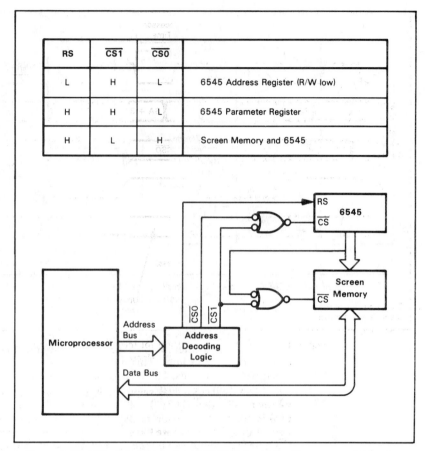

RS	CS1	CS0	
L	H	L	6545 Address Register (R/W low)
H	H	L	6545 Parameter Register
H	L	H	Screen Memory and 6545

Figure 5-11. Chip Select Logic for 6545 CRT Controller Transparent Addressing

microprocessor selects screen memory (as an I/O port), it also causes a select signal to be sent to the 6545 to address the Update register-pair. In addition, this mode of operation will require the same multi-step sequence to prepare for the transfer of a first byte of data, but subsequent transfers require only a single cycle so long as consecutive screen memory locations are being accessed.

Therefore, you should refer to our earlier discussion of chip select logic and the preliminary steps required to load the Update register-pair for a discussion of these set-up conditions.

The one significant difference between Figure 5-12 and Figure 5-9, which showed the configuration for interleaved transparent addressing, **is the addition of a data hold latch between screen memory and the microprocessor. The latch will be required since the microprocessor will not always have immediate access to screen memory; therefore the latch is used to hold data temporarily.** The Update Strobe (UPSTB) signal from the 6545 is used to load data into the latch from screen memory, or to gate data written into the latch by the microprocessor into screen memory.

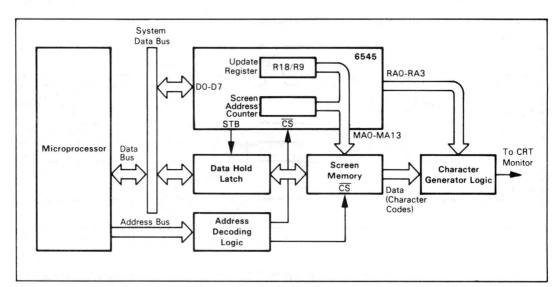

Figure 5-12. 6545 CRT Controller Transparent Memory Addressing Configuration for Retrace Mode

Figure 5-13 shows the timing for the UPSTB signal. As soon as a non-display interval is entered, the 6545 outputs the contents of the update register on the MA0-MA13 lines. This update address will be output for 3 Character Clock (CCLK) periods. The UPSTB pulse is 1 CCLK period in duration and is centered within the update address interval.

The timing illustrated in Figure 5-13 shows how data already loaded into the holding latch would be strobed into screen memory at the appropriate time. **This timing does not, however, illustrate how the microprocessor can determine when it can load another byte of data into the latch. This is where the Ready bit in the 6545 status register comes into play.**

Ready Status Bit

Figure 5-14 illustrates the operation of bit 7, the Ready bit, in the 6545's Status register. When the 6545 is first powered-up, bit 7 will be set to a 1. Whenever you load a byte of data into the data latch, you must simultaneously access register R31 within the 6545 device. This access causes the Ready bit to be reset. When the 6545 subsequently enters a non-display interval, it outputs the update address and generates the UPSTB signal to load that data into screen memory. Two CCLK periods later, the Ready bit will once again be set high by the 6545. The microprocessor must then poll the 6545 device, by reading the contents of the Status register, to check the state of the Ready bit. If this bit is low, it means that new data from screen memory has not yet been loaded into the latch. When this bit is set high, it indicates that data from screen memory has been loaded into the latch and can be read from the latch by the microprocessor. When the microprocessor subsequently issues a read to the data latch, the read operation should also access register R31 in the 6545. The operation will both capture data from the latch and increment the contents of the 6545's Update register so that the next consecutive screen memory location can be accessed. The Ready bit in the Status register will be

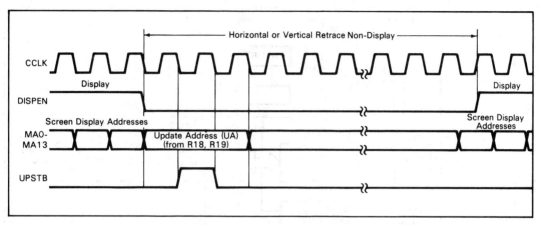

Figure 5-13. 6545 CRT Controller Update Strobe (UPSTB) Timing

reset by this access of register R31. Thus, the Ready bit in the Status register indicates to the microprocessor when data is available, while the UPSTB signal from the 6545 effects the transfer of addressed data from refresh memory into the data latch.

While the chip select logic required for this mode of operation is quite similar to that of the interleaved transparent addressing mode, there are minor differences. For example, a read operation initiated by the microprocessor must cause a chip select signal or buffer enable signal to be generated for the data latch, instead of for screen memory, while it simultaneously selects the 6545 to access register R31.

The timing for successive write operations in this transparent mode of operation during non-display portions is not quite as straightforward as with read operations. Figure 5-15 illustrates the sequence for two successive write operations. Successive write operations effectively cause a double update cycle, since read operations are automatically initiated by the 6545 and interleaved with each of the write operations. As you can see, the contents of the Update register-pair will only be incremented by the occurrence of UPSTB after register R31 has been accessed as part of a microprocessor-initiated write operation. **The 6545 operates in this way so that a byte of data is always available from screen memory in the data latch, should the microprocessor perform a read operation.** If instead, the microprocessor performs a write operation, data that was previously read from screen memory is simply ignored. **The microprocessor must still poll the 6545 by reading the contents of the Status register to determine the state of the Ready bit.** In this case, when the Ready status bit is low, it indicates that the 6545 is waiting to store data held in the data latch in the location addressed by the contents of the Update register-pair. When the Ready status bit goes high, it indicates that data held in the latch has been written into screen memory and the microprocessor can then send another byte of data to the latch.

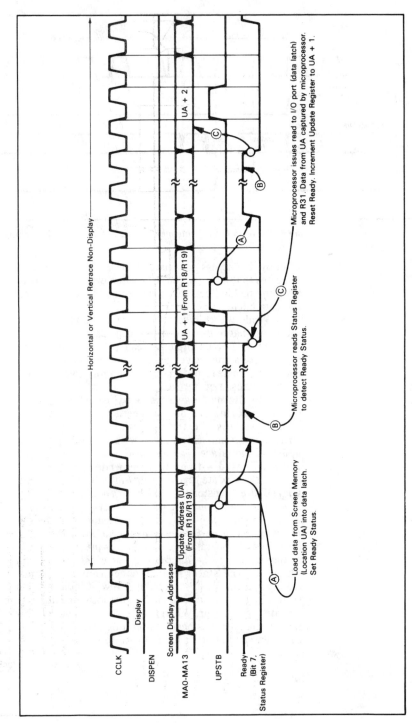

Figure 5-14. 6545 Ready Status Timing for Successive Read Operations

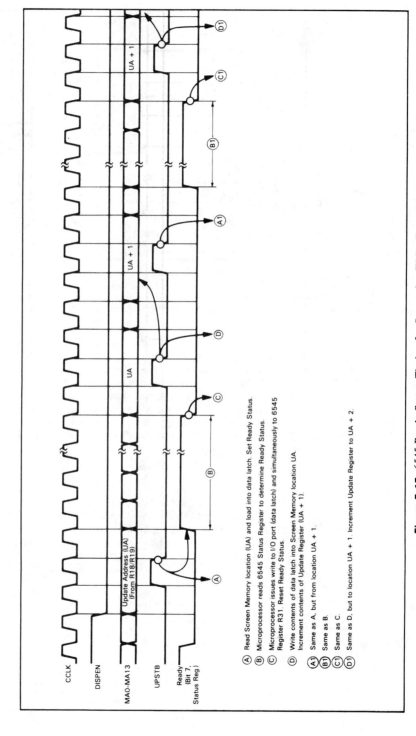

Ⓐ Read Screen Memory location (UA) and load into data latch. Set Ready Status.

Ⓑ Microprocessor reads 6545 Status Register to determine Ready Status.

Ⓒ Microprocessor issues write to I/O port (data latch) and simultaneously to 6545 Register R31. Reset Ready Status.

Ⓓ Write contents of data latch into Screen Memory location UA. Increment contents of Update Register (UA + 1).

Ⓐ₁ Same as A, but from location UA + 1.

Ⓑ₁ Same as B.

Ⓒ₁ Same as C.

Ⓓ₁ Same as D, but to location UA + 1. Increment Update Register to UA + 2.

Figure 5-15. 6545 Ready Status Timing for Successive Write Operations

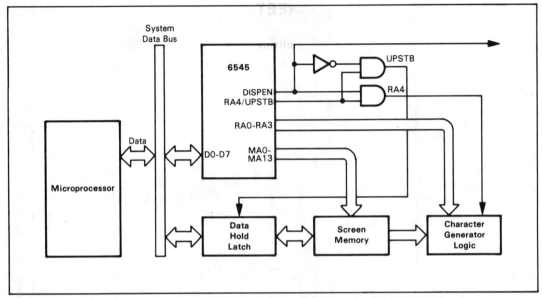

Figure 5-16. Using the 6545 CRT Controller's Dual-Function RA4/UPSTB Signal

As you can deduce from the timing in Figure 5-15, the hardware required to implement the data latch is not quite as straightforward as implied by the timing for read operations. The data latch must also include some way of storing the fact that the microprocessor performed a write into the latch. Then, a following update strobe can gate data from the latch into screen memory and supply the required write signal to memory at the time of the UPSTB strobe.

When you are using the 6545 in the retrace-transparent-addressing mode, you can utilize both functions of the RA4/UPSTB signal and thus achieve character sizes greater than the 16 scan line limit that is imposed if you use only RA0-RA3. Internally, the 6545 generates the RA4 and UPSTB signals separately; it simply uses the same pin to output the two signals. During non-display (retrace) intervals, the internal RA4 signal is always low. If the retrace-transparent-addressing mode has been specified, UPSTB will be output during retrace intervals. The DISPEN signal will always be low during retrace and thus can be used to reconstruct the separate RA4 and UPSTB signals external to the 6545. Figure 5-16 shows the external logic needed to create separate RA4 and UPSTB signals. With the logic shown, RA4 will only be active during display times and disabled during retrace times, while UPSTB will only function during retrace or non-display times.

DATA SHEETS

This section contains specific eletrical and timing data for the 6545.

6545

MAXIMUM RATINGS

Supply Voltage, V_{CC}	-0.3V to +7.0V
Input/Output Voltage, V_{IN}	-0.3V to +7.0V
Operating Temperature, T_{OP}	$0°C$ to $70°C$
Storage Temperature, T_{STG}	$-55°C$ to $150°C$

All inputs contain protection circuitry to prevent damage due to high static discharges. Care should be exercised to prevent unnecessary application of voltages in excess of the allowable limits.

COMMENT

Stresses above those listed under "Absolute Maximum Ratings" may cause permanent damage to the device. These are stress ratings only. Functional operation of this device at these or any other conditions above those indicated in the operational sections of this specification is not implied and exposure to absolute maximum rating conditions for extended periods may affect device reliability.

ELECTRICAL CHARACTERISTICS (V_{CC} = 5.0V ± 5%, T_A = 0-70°C, unless otherwise noted)

Symbol	Characteristic	Min.	Max.	Unit
V_{IH}	Input High Voltage	2.0	V_{CC}	V
V_{IL}	Input Low Voltage	-0.3	0.8	V
I_{IN}	Input Leakage ($\phi2$, R/$\overline{w}$, $\overline{RES}$, $\overline{CS}$, RS, LPEN, CCLK)	–	2.5	μA
I_{TSI}	Three-State Input Leakage (DB0-DB7) V_{IN} = 0.4 to 2.4V	–	10.0	μA
V_{OH}	Output High Voltage I_{LOAD} = 205μA (DB0-DB7) I_{LOAD} = 100μA (all others)	2.4	–	V
V_{OL}	Output Low Voltage I_{LOAD} = 1.6mA	–	0.4	V
P_D	Power Dissipation	–	800	mW
C_{IN}	Input Capacitance $\phi2$, R/$\overline{w}$, $\overline{RES}$, $\overline{CS}$, RS, LPEN, CCLK DB0-DB7	– –	10.0 12.5	pF pF
C_{OUT}	Output Capacitance	–	10.0	pF

TEST LOAD

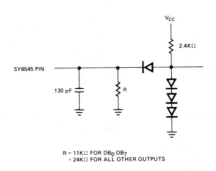

V_{CC}

2.4KΩ

SY6545 PIN

130 pF

R

R = 11KΩ FOR DB$_0$-DB$_7$
= 24KΩ FOR ALL OTHER OUTPUTS

6545

MPU BUS INTERFACE CHARACTERISTICS

WRITE CYCLE

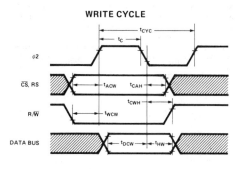

READ CYCLE

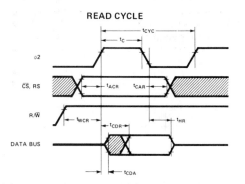

WRITE TIMING CHARACTERISTICS (V_{CC} = 5.0V ± 5%, T_A = 0–70°C, unless otherwise noted)

Symbol	Characteristic	SY6545		SY6545A		Unit
		Min.	Max.	Min.	Max.	
t_{CYC}	Cycle Time	1.0	–	0.5	–	μs
t_C	ϕ2 Pulse Width	470	–	235	–	ns
t_{ACW}	Address Set-Up Time	180	–	90	–	ns
t_{CAH}	Address Hold Time	0	–	0	–	ns
t_{WCW}	R/$\overline{W}$ Set-Up Time	180	–	90	–	ns
t_{CWH}	R/$\overline{W}$ Hold Time	0	–	0	–	ns
t_{DCW}	Data Bus Set-Up Time	300	–	150	–	ns
t_{HW}	Data Bus Hold Time	10	–	10	–	ns

(t_r and t_f = 10 to 30 ns)

READ TIMING CHARACTERISTICS (V_{CC} = 5.0V ± 5%, T_A = 0–70°C, unless otherwise noted)

Symbol	Characteristic	SY6545		SY6545A		Unit
		Min.	Max.	Min.	Max.	
t_{CYC}	Cycle Time	1.0	–	0.5	–	μs
t_C	ϕ2 Pulse Width	470	–	235	–	ns
t_{ACR}	Address Set-Up Time	180	–	90	–	ns
t_{CAR}	Address Hold Time	0	–	0	–	ns
t_{WCR}	R/$\overline{W}$ Set-Up Time	180	–	90	–	ns
t_{CDR}	Read Access Time (Valid Data)	–	395	–	200	ns
t_{HR}	Read Hold Time	10	–	10	–	ns
t_{CDA}	Data Bus Active Time (Invalid Data)	40	–	40	–	ns

(t_r and t_f = 10 to 30 ns)

6545

MEMORY AND VIDEO INTERFACE CHARACTERISTICS
(V_{CC} = 5.0V ± 5%, T_A = 0 to 70°C, unless otherwise noted)

SYSTEM TIMING

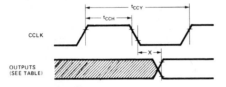

Output	Parameter
MA0-MA13	t_{MAD}
RA0-RA4	t_{RAD}
DISPLAY-ENABLE	t_{DTD}
HSYNC	t_{HSD}
VSYNC	t_{VSD}
CURSOR	t_{CDD}

Symbol	Characteristic	SY6545 Min.	SY6545 Max.	SY6545A Min.	SY6545A Max.	Unit
t_{CCY}	Character Clock Cycle Time	0.40	40	0.40	40	µs
t_{CCH}	Character Clock Pulse Width	200	—	200	—	ns
t_{MAD}	MA0-MA13 Propagation Delay	—	160	—	160	ns
t_{RAD}	RA0-RA4 Propagation Delay	—	160	—	160	ns
t_{DTD}	DISPLAY ENABLE Propagation Delay	—	300	—	300	ns
t_{HSD}	HSYNC Propagation Delay	—	300	—	300	ns
t_{VSD}	VSYNC Propagation Delay	—	300	—	300	ns
t_{CDD}	CURSOR Propagation Delay	—	300	—	300	ns

LIGHT PEN STROBE TIMING

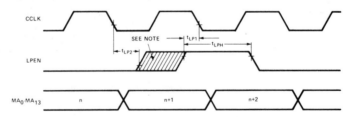

NOTE: "Safe" time position for LPEN positive edge to cause
address n+2 to load into Light Pen Register.
t_{LP2} and t_{LP1} are time positions causing uncertain results.

Symbol	Characteristic	SY6545 Min.	SY6545 Max.	SY6545A Min.	SY6545A Max.	Unit
t_{LPH}	LPEN Strobe Width	100	—	100	—	ns
t_{LP1}	LPEN to CCLK Delay	120	—	120	—	ns
t_{LP2}	CCLK to LPEN Delay	0	—	0	—	ns

t_r, t_f = 20 ns (max)

6

The 5027 CRT Controller

The 5027 CRT controller was one of the first of the LSI controller devices introduced. The functions provided by the 5027 may appear to be somewhat more elementary than those available with devices introduced more recently. Nonetheless, the 5027 still provides several interesting functions not available on any of the other devices we have described.

Figure 6-1 shows those portions of the idealized CRT controller, which we developed in Chapter 1, that are provided by the 5027. If you compare this figure to the equivalent ones for other CRT controllers we have described, it may appear that the amount of logic provided by the 5027 is approximately equal to that provided by the other devices. However, as we shall see when we describe the logic of the 5027 in detail, many of the functions are implemented in a minimal fashion. For example, Figure 6-1 indicates that cursor logic is provided on the 5027, but the logic provided simply generates a continuous stream of dots at a specified cursor location. You cannot cause the cursor to automatically blink, nor do you have any options in specifying the shape of the cursor symbol as was the case with some other CRT controllers. We should note that this will not necessarily be a disadvantage since many character generators (for example, the 8002, a companion part to the 5027) can provide the logic necessary to create different types of cursor symbols.

On the other hand, the SYNC generation logic provided by the 5027 exceeds that which is provided by most of the other devices. Not only are HSYNC and VSYNC generated by the device, but a composite synchronization (CSYNC) signal is also available.

The 5027 provides no memory contention logic to simplify access to screen memory by both the microprocessor and the CRT controller. In addition, the screen memory addressing logic provided by the 5027 always addresses screen memory on a row/column basis; it cannot generate linear memory addresses.

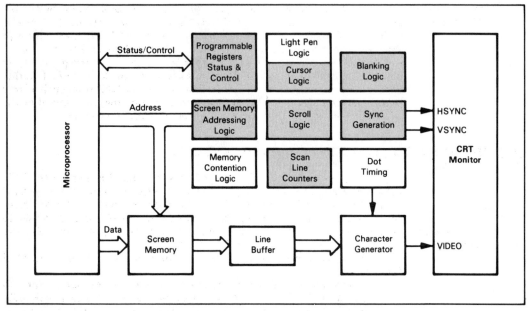

Figure 6-1. 5027 CRT Controller Functional Logic

One unique feature of the 5027 which is not indicated in Figure 6-1 is a self-load capability which allows the device to be semi-automatically initialized during startup time.

The primary manufacturer of the 5027 CRT controller is:

SMC MICROSYSTEMS CORPORATION
35 Marcus Boulevard
Hauppauge, NY 11787

Second sources for the 5027 are:

TEXAS INSTRUMENTS, INC.
P.O. Box 225012
Dallas, TX 75265

SOLID STATE SCIENTIFIC, INC.
Montgomeryville Industrial Center
Montgomeryville, PA 18936

MOSTEK CORPORATION
1215 West Crosby Road
Carrollton, TX 75006

**The TMS9927
CRT Controller**   The device produced by SMC Microsystems, Solid State Scientific, and Mostek is designated the 5027, while the Texas Instruments device is called the TMS9927. The two devices are functionally identical although there are minor differences in signal nomenclature. Throughout this chapter we shall simply refer to this CRT controller as the 5027 except where we point out minor differences in signal naming conventions. It is worth noting here that no other device described in this book is available from such a large number of manufacturers. This is due both to the length of time that the 5027 has been in existence, and to its wide use and acceptance.

THE 5027 CRT CONTROLLER PINS AND SIGNALS

Figure 6-2 shows the pin assignments and signal names for the 5027 CRT controller. The signals may be divided into three categories: signals used to interface the CRT controller to the microprocessor and system busses (standard power and timing input signals are included in this group), signals used to

**Microprocessor
Interface Signals**   interface the controller to screen memory and character generator logic, and signals directly related to the CRT monitor.

The microprocessor-CRT controller interface signals are described below.

CS is a standard Chip Select signal and must be set high in order to access one of the 5027's internal registers or to issue a command to the 5027.

A0-A3 are the register/command address inputs and determine which of the 5027's internal registers will accessed or which of the commands recognized by the 5027 is to be executed.

$\overline{DS}$ is the Data Strobe input and must be pulsed low to accomplish a register access or command initiation. Note that the 5027 has no read or write control signal inputs; the $\overline{DS}$ signal is the functional combination of RD and WR signals.

DB0-DB7 are the Data Bus lines used to exchange 8-bit parallel bytes of information between the 5027 and the microprocessor system. These eight lines are bidirectional pins used as inputs to the control registers of the 5027 and outputs from the cursor address registers of the 5027. You will note in Figure 6-2 that the 9927 device labels the most significant bit of the data bus as DB0, and the least significant bit as DB7. This convention is used in all devices made by Texas Instruments but is the opposite of that used by most manufacturers. Throughout this chapter, we will use the more standard convention, with DB0 representing the least significant bit and DB7 the most significant bit.

DCC is the Dot Counter Carry input signal used to time all of the internal operations of the 5027. This is the character rate clock signal derived from external dot timing logic; thus it is not truly a microprocesser system interface signal, but is more closely associated with the video and character generator logic. Nonetheless, we have grouped it with the other microprocessor interface signals since it is the primary timing input to the 5027 device.

V_{CC} (+5 V), V_{DD} (+12 V) and GND are standard power and ground connections. The 5027 device is the only controller described in this book which requires both +5 V and +12 V. This will not necessarily be a disadvantage since most terminals will have +12 V, which is needed for an RS-232 interface.

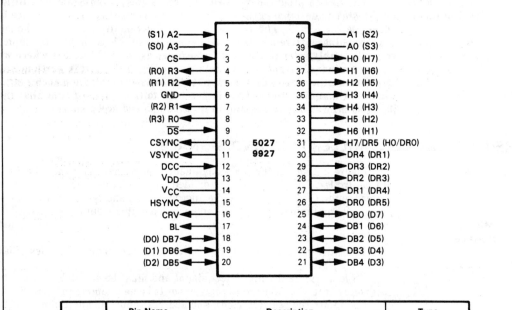

	Pin Name	Description	Type
Microprocessor System Interface Signals	CS	Chip Select	Input
	A0-A3	Register Address	Input
	$\overline{DS}$	Data Strobe	Input
	DB0-DB7	Data Bus Lines	Bidirectional
	DCC	Dot Counter Carry (Character Clock)	Input
	V_{CC}, V_{DD}, GND	Power Supplies (+5 V, +12 V) and Ground	Input
Screen Memory and Character Generator Signals	H0-H6	Horizontal (Character Counter) Outputs	Output
	H7/DR5	Horizontal Count Output/Data Row Output	Output
	DR0-DR4	Data Row Counter Outputs	Output
	R0-R3	Scan Line Counter Outputs	Output
CRT Monitor Interface Signals	HSYNC	Horizontal Synchronization	Output
	VSYNC	Vertical Synchronization	Output
	CSYNC	Composite Synchronization	Output
	CRV	Cursor Video	Output
	BL	Blanking Signal	Output

Figure 6-2. 5027 CRT Controller Pins and Signals

There are two sets of signals associated with screen memory addressing logic (H0-H7, DR0-DR5) and one set of signals associated with character generator logic (R0-R3).

Screen Memory and Character Generator Signals

The 5027 addresses screen memory on a column/row basis. H0-H7 are the horizontal character or column address outputs, and DR0-DR5 are the vertical or data row address outputs. Pin number 31 functions as the most significant column output (H7) if required; otherwise it is the most significant data row output (DR5). While this gives you some flexibility in utilizing memory address space, this column/row addressing method will still result in inefficient use of memory space in most cases. For a discussion of the advantages and disadvantages of row/column addressing versus linear memory addressing refer to Chapter 1.

R0-R3 are the Raster or scan line counter outputs which will be used as inputs to character generator logic to select the proper dot pattern for the various scan lines comprising each character row.

The 5027 provides a fairly standard set of signals to implement the CRT monitor interface. HSYNC and VSYNC are the standard Horizontal Synchronization and Vertical Synchronization signals. The position and duration of these signals is programmable and is established by loading the desired values into the 5027's control registers.

CRT Monitor Signals

CSYNC is the Composite Synchronization signal and outputs a pulse stream which includes both the HSYNC and CSYNC signals. The CSYNC signal can only be used if the 5027 is operating in the non-interlaced mode (we will discuss interlaced and non-interlaced modes later in this chapter). The CSYNC signal can be externally mixed with video to produce a composite video output to the CRT monitor.

CRV is the Cursor Video output signal. The 5027 has two cursor position registers which can be loaded under program control. When the screen memory address is the same as the address defined by the cursor position registers, then the CRV signal will be set high to produce a continuous stream of dots at that character position. The CRV signal will be set high at that character position for all scan lines comprising the character row. Thus, **the cursor symbol produced by the 5027 will always appear as a block signal as opposed to an underline cursor symbol.** However, external logic may be utilized to generate other cursor types using CRV as a condition signal.

BL is the Blanking signal and will be output high during vertical and horizontal retrace. BL will also be high during those portions of horizontal and vertical scan where video data is not to be displayed. You establish those times when BL is to be active under program control by loading the desired values into the control registers.

Table 6-1. 5027 CRT Controller Registers and Command Summary

Address				Read (R) or Write (W)	Control Reg. #	Register/Command Function
A3	A2	A1	A0			
0	0	0	0	W	0	Load Horizontal Character Count Register
0	0	0	1	W	1	Load HSYNC Width/Delay Register. Set Interlace Mode
0	0	1	0	W	2	Load Characters and Scan Lines Per Data Row Register
0	0	1	1	W	3	Load Data Rows Per Frame and Skew Register
0	1	0	0	W	4	Load Scan Lines Per Frame Register
0	1	0	1	W	5	Load Vertical Data Start Register
0	1	1	0	W	6	Load Last Displayed Data Row Register
0	1	1	1	X		Set Processor Self-Load Mode
1	0	0	0	R		Read Cursor Row Address
1	0	0	1	R		Read Cursor Character Address
1	0	1	0	X		Reset
1	0	1	1	X		Up Scroll
1	1	0	0	W		Load Cursor Character Address
1	1	0	1	W		Load Cursor Row Address
1	1	1	0	X		Start Timing Chain
1	1	1	1	X		Non-Processor Self-Load

X = don't care

THE 5027 CRT CONTROLLER PROGRAMMABLE REGISTERS

The 5027 provides nine internal registers which are illustrated in Figure 6-3. Seven of the registers (control registers 0-6) are used to define timing parameters and screen format, and the remaining two registers define the screen location where the cursor symbol is to be displayed. Address inputs A0-A3 specify which of the registers is to be accessed. Table 6-1 lists the 5027's registers, their functions, and the address assignments for each.

When the register address inputs (A0-A3) are applied to the 5027 and accompanied by the CS and $\overline{DS}$ signals, the 5027 decodes the address inputs to generate the appropriate register select signals. As you can see in Figure 6-3 and Table 6-1, the register address inputs are also used to issue commands to the 5027. Actually, the register address inputs might more accurately be viewed simply as command inputs; some of the commands cause data to be loaded into the control registers while other commands do not operate on these registers but instead cause other control functions (such as reset) to be initiated.

The seven control registers are write-only registers. When they are selected, the data that is to be written into the registers must be present on DB0-DB7 when the Data Strobe ($\overline{DS}$) signal is applied. The two cursor position registers are read/write registers: you write data into the registers to position the cursor on the screen and you can read the contents of the registers to ascertain the current cursor position. Since the 5027 provides no signal to differentiate between register read and write operations, two separate addresses are used to access each of these cursor registers: one address is used for write operations and another during read operations.

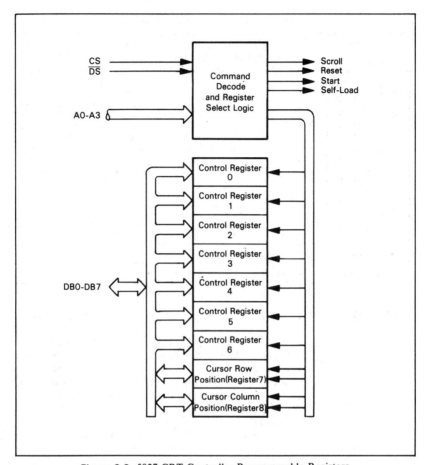

Figure 6-3. 5027 CRT Controller Programmable Registers

Since the seven control registers are used to establish basic screen format and timing characterstics, they will usually be loaded when a system is first started up and will not have to be accessed thereafter. It is only the cursor position registers that will be accessed on any recurring basis.

Since the contents of the control registers determine all of the primary operating characteristics of the 5027, we will defer a description of the contents of each register until later in this chapter when we describe programming the device.

THE 5027-MICROPROCESSOR SYSTEM INTERFACE

The interface that the 5027 presents to the microprocessor system is, for the most part, quite straightforward. The signals used to interface the controller to the microprocessor consist of the eight Data Bus lines (DB0-DB7), the Chip Select (CS) signal, the register address inputs (A0-A3), and the Data Strobe ($\overline{DS}$) signal.

Figure 6-4 illustrates, in a simplified form, the interface between the 5027 and the microprocessor system. Data is passed between the 5027 and the microprocessor via the eight bidirectional data lines (DB0-DB7). The timing for a microprocessor write operation to load data into one of the 5027s internal registers or to initiate one of the commands can be illustrated as follows:

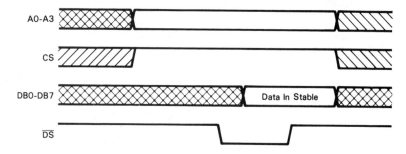

Read/Write Operations

The register address inputs (A0-A3) must be stable and the Chip Select (CS) signal must be high before the Data Strobe ($\overline{DS}$) signal is driven low. As we have indicated in Figure 6-3, the $\overline{DS}$ signal would typically be the logical NOR of the microprocessor-generated Read (RD) and Write (WR) signals. The timing requirements for $\overline{DS}$, so far as pulse width is concerned, are identical whether you are writing data into the 5027 or reading information from the 5027. Data that is to be loaded into the 5027 must be presented on the DB0-DB7 lines some minimal time interval before $\overline{DS}$ makes its negative-to-positive transition, and the data must be held stable until after that transition.

The timing for a read operation initiated by the microprocessor to read the contents of one of the 5027's cursor position registers is equally straightforward and can be illustrated as follows:

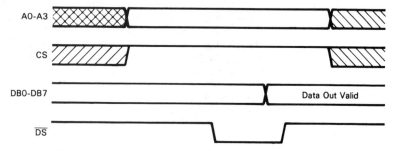

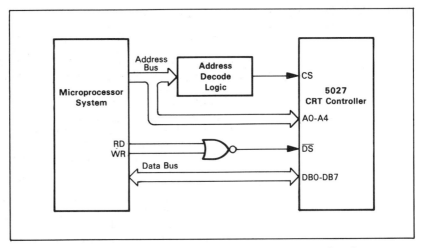

Figure 6-4. 5027 CRT Controller-Microprocessor System Interface

If you refer once again to Figure 6-3 you will note that both the Chip Select (CS) and register address (A0-A3) inputs to the 5027 are derived from the microprocessor system's address bus. Thus the 5027 would occupy 16 memory or I/O locations in the microprocessor system's addressing space. Each register/command of the 5027 would thus be addressed by the microprocessor as a separate memory location or I/O device. Data can be written to nine of these locations (the seven control registers and the two cursor position registers) and read from two of these locations (the cursor position registers). The remaining five addresses initiate commands, and no transfer of data is required; for these commands, the microprocessor could simply perform a dummy access to that command address location.

When the system is first powered up, a succession of write operations must be directed to the 5027 in order to establish initial values in all of the control registers. This initialization process can be accomplished using microprocessor-initiated write operations as we have just described. There are two other methods of establishing these initial control register values for the 5027. First, if volume justifies it, you can order mask-programmed versions of the 5027 which will have the values that you specify permanently set into the control registers. For example, the 5047 device produced by SMC Microsystems has a fixed format of 24 data rows with 80 characters per row. It is thus the functional equivalent of the pre-programmed DP8350 described in Chapter 2. With one of these pre-programmed versions, the microprocessor would only need to access the 5027 to load the cursor registers or read the contents of the cursor position registers. Of course, this approach permanently fixes the operating characteristics of the 5027.

The 5027 CRT Controller Self-Load Operation

Another method of establishing initial values for the control registers in the 5027 is to use the self-load capability of the device. Figure 6-5 shows, in a generalized form, the logic configuration required for the self-load operation. An external PROM device is used to store the values that are to be loaded into the 5027's control registers and cursor position registers. Although only nine bytes will be required to load the registers, we have shown a 32×8 PROM since that is the smallest such device widely available. During the self-load operation, the address inputs to the PROM will be supplied by the 5027 via its raster address (R0-R3) outputs.

The self-load operation is initiated by presenting the command (1111_2) on the A0-A3 inputs to the 5027. The CS input must also be high. The self-load operation begins when the $\overline{\text{DS}}$ signal is pulsed. Thus the system initialization logic must be capable of producing a signal (named $\overline{\text{SLOAD}}$ in Figure 6-5) which will select the 5027 and present the self-load command on the address inputs. This external logic must also generate the $\overline{\text{DS}}$ pulse. Once the self-load command has been initiated, the 5027 will begin outputting the PROM addresses on the R0-R3 lines. The first seven addresses output will be 0000_2 through 0110_2 and the data output from the PROM for each of these address locations will be loaded by the 5027 into its seven control registers (R0-R6). When the scan counter outputs are 0111_2 and 1000_2, the PROM data that is accessed will be loaded into the Cursor Character Address register and Cursor Row Address register respectively. Note that these last two scan counter output addresses do not correspond to the Cursor Position register addresses defined in Table 6-1.

The A0-A3 and CS inputs to the 5027 must be held high for the duration of the self-load operation. The time required for this operation will depend on the frequency at which the 5027 is being operated; that is, the DCC or character clock input frequency to the device. The R0-R3 outputs which are used to address the PROM are incremented at the HSYNC frequency. After all of the required values have been read from PROM and loaded into the 5027, the timing chain of the 5027 is initiated by removal of the "all ones" state from the A0-A3 inputs; this initiation is independent of the state of the $\overline{\text{DS}}$ input.

The self-load operation we have just described is the non-processor self-load procedure. The processor-initiated self-load is identical to this procedure except that the command code is 0111_2 and the timing chain is not automatically initiated when the command code is removed from the A0-A3 inputs. Instead, the processor must issue the Start Timing Chain command in order to place the 5027 into full operation.

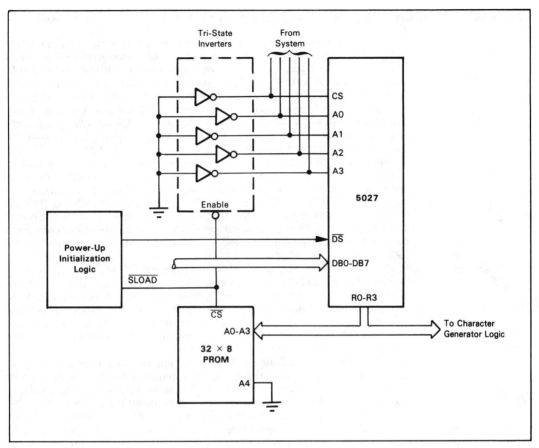

Figure 6-5. 5027 CRT Controller Self-Load Logic

THE 5027-SCREEN MEMORY/CHARACTER GENERATOR INTERFACE

The only signals that the 5027 device provides specifically for the screen memory interface are the eight horizontal character count outputs (H0-H7) and the five vertical or data row counter outputs (DR0-DR4). Thus, 13 address outputs are available to access screen memory. With 13 lines, you can address up to 8K of memory; however, because the 5027 addresses memory on a row/column basis instead of using straight linear addressing, you would only be able to address this maximum amount of screen memory if the screen were comprised of 32 rows (DR0-DR4) of 256 characters each (H0-H7) or of 64 rows (DR0-DR5) with 128 characters each (H0-H6). However, you do not have complete flexibility in defining the number of characters per row, as we will see when we discuss programming the control registers. Therefore, the size of screen memory that the 5027 can address will be more rigidly limited than was the case with any of the other CRT controllers. In addition, the row/column approach to memory addressing, while well suited for manipulation of screen data, can result in inefficient use of memory. For a discussion of the advantages and disadvantages of row/column memory addressing, refer to Chapter 1.

Figure 6-6 shows the relationship between the 5027 CRT controller, screen memory, and character generator logic. One significant aspect of this illustration is the fact that the 5027 provides no logic to deal with memory contention resolution: external logic must be provided to determine when the microprocessor can use the address bus to access screen memory and when the 5027 can use its H0-H7 and DR0-DR4 outputs to access screen memory. You may need to decode the R0-R3 outputs from the 5027 to determine those scan lines when the device will not require access to screen memory, or you may be able to use the BL (Blanking) signal to enable microprocessor access to screen memory. You should refer to the discussions of memory contention resolution logic in Chapter 1 for additional details. The point we are making here is that the 5027 provides no logic to specifically aid you in designing external circuitry for memory contention resolution.

Character Generator Interface Logic   The interface that the 5027 provides to character generator logic simply consists of the four raster address or scan line counter outputs (R0-R3). These outputs comprise one set of inputs to the character generator logic, while the data from screen memory comprises the second set of character code inputs to character generator logic. The R0-R3 outputs can represent scan line counts ranging from 1 to 16, and thus character rows can be comprised of up to 16 scan lines. If you are using the 5027 in the interlaced mode, R0 also serves as the odd or even field indicator. You can still have up to 16 scan lines in this mode, however. Operating in the interlaced mode allows you to double the density of information on the screen but may result in screen flicker. For a further discussion of interlaced modes refer to the general discussion in Chapter 1 and the description of the interlaced modes of the 6845 in Chapter 4.

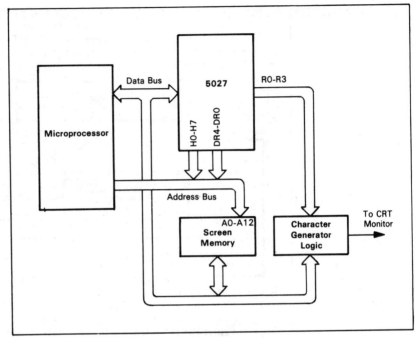

Figure 6-6. 5027 CRT Controller Interface to Screen Memory/Character
Generator Logic

THE 5027-CRT MONITOR INTERFACE

Figure 6-7 illustrates the signals provided by the 5027 to implement the
interface to a CRT monitor. The signals provided are quite comparable to those
provided by the 6845 and the 6545 controllers described in Chapters 4 and 5.

**The Horizontal Synchronization (HSYNC) and Vertical Synchroniza-
tion (VSYNC) signals are the standard signals compatible with 3-terminal
CRT monitors.** You specify the exact time when these pulses are to be generated by loading the appropriate values into the control registers. The duration
of the HSYNC pulse is also programmed-specified. The VSYNC pulse,
however, is of a fixed duration (3 scan line times) and thus external logic may
be required to obtain a VSYNC pulse of the proper duration for a given CRT
monitor. It should be noted, however, that this 3-scan-line pulse does meet the
requirements of the EIA RS-170 video specification and would allow you to
operate with most CRT's.

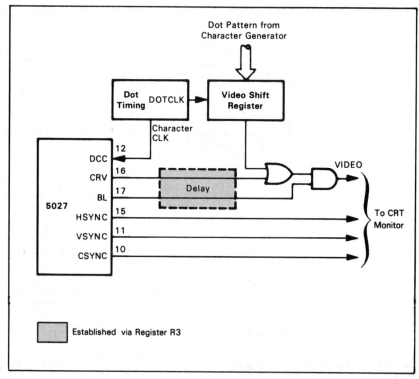

Figure 6-7. 5027 CRT Controller-CRT Monitor Interface

The Composite Synchronization (CSYNC) output combines both the HSYNC and VSYNC signals for CRT monitors that can use such an input. The way in which HSYNC and VSYNC are combined in the Composite Synchronization output can be illustrated as follows:

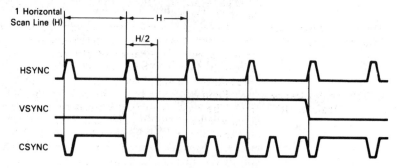

The Cursor Video (CRV) signal is generated by the 5027 whenever the screen memory address is equal to the address contained in the cursor position registers. This signal is similar to that provided by the other CRT controller devices we described but it is limited in that there are no programmable options provided to create cursors of different shapes or blinking cursor

symbols. The CRV signal will simply be output high during all scan lines at the cursor position, thus creating a block cursor symbol. You can, of course, use external logic to create a reverse video cursor symbol.

The Blanking (BL) signal will be set high during horizontal and vertical retrace times and thus can be used to turn off VIDEO during these intervals. You specify those points where the BL signal is to be activated by loading the appropriate values into the control registers. Those intervals where BL is to be activated have no fixed relationships to the occurrence of the HSYNC or VSYNC signals. Instead, **the BL signal will be activated at all times except during those intervals when you have specified that characters are to be displayed on the screen.**

The CRV, BL, and HSYNC signals are all synchronized to the screen memory address outputs: that is, when the screen address corresponding to the cursor position, start of blanking, or HSYN activation point is generated, then the CRV, BL, or HSYN signal will be activiated at that time. **However,** since some time will be required to access the corresponding character from screen memory, generate the dot pattern very via character generator logic and shifted out the the video shift register, **the CRV, BL, or HSYN signal may be activated well before the corresponding character is being sent to the screen. This effect is known as "pipelining"** and we have discussed it in relationship to other CRT controllers. **The 5027 allows you to introduce skew delays to account for this pipelining effect by programming the appropriate control register.** In Figure 6-7 we have indicated this programmable delay function for these three signals with the dotted block across CRV, BL, and HSYNC. Delays of one or two character times can be specified for each of these signals.

PROGRAMMING THE 5027 CRT CONTROLLER REGISTERS

The 5027 provides seven control registers which must be loaded when the device is first powered up to establish basic operating parameters for the device. As you will recall from our earlier discussion of the programmable registers, **the register address inputs (A0-A3) are also used to issue commands to the 5027. At this point we will limit our discussion to programming of the control registers and we will discuss the commands executed by the 5027 separately.**

Horizontal Character Count Register (R0)

Figure 6-8 shows the format for the Horizontal Character Count register (R0). The contents of this register determine the total time allotted for one scan line in terms of character clock times (DCC). This register defines the total time for a horizontal scan line including the horizontal retrace time and thus determines the HSYNC frequency.

HSYNC Width/Decay Register (R1)

Figure 6-9 shows the format for the HSYNC Width/Delay register (R1). The least significant 3 bits define the HSYNC delay. This delay is frequently called the front porch and is a period between the end of active video on a scan line and the leading edge of the HSYNC pulse. This delay thus positions the displayed portion horizontally on the CRT screen. **Bits 3 through 6 specify the duration or width of the HSYNC pulse. HSYNC can be up to 15 character clocks (DCC) in duration.**

The most significant bit of register R1 is used to specify whether the 5027 is to operate in the interlaced or non-interlaced mode. You should refer to our earlier discussion of the interlaced mode for additional details of the effects of this specification.

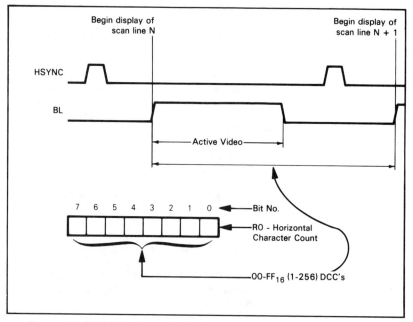

Figure 6-8. 5027 CRT Controller Horizontal Character Count Register (R0)

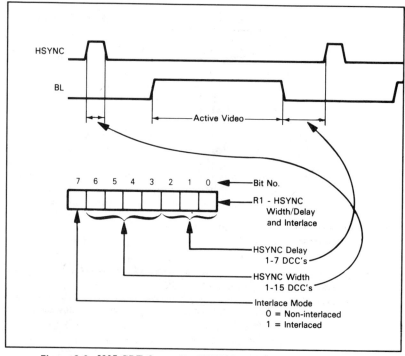

Figure 6-9. 5027 CRT Controller HSYNC Width/Delay Register (R1)

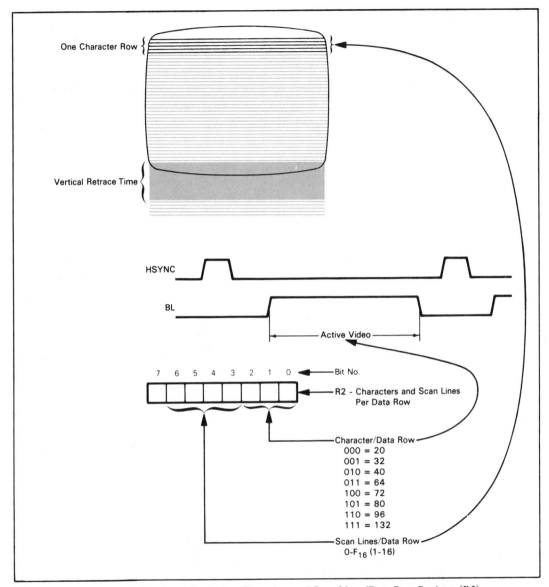

Figure 6-10. 5027 CRT Controller Characters and Scan Lines/Data Row Register (R2)

**Character and Scan
Lines Per Data Row
Register (R2)**

Figure 6-10 shows the format for the Character and Scan Lines Per Data Row register (R2). The least significant three bits specify the number of characters per data row that are to be displayed. As you can see, you have eight possible choices ranging from 20 to 132 characters per data row. If you specify a mask-programmed version of the 5027, however, you can obtain up to 200 characters per row. The next four bits (3-6) of this register determine the number of scan lines that shall comprise each data row. A character row can consist of from 1 to 16 scan lines.

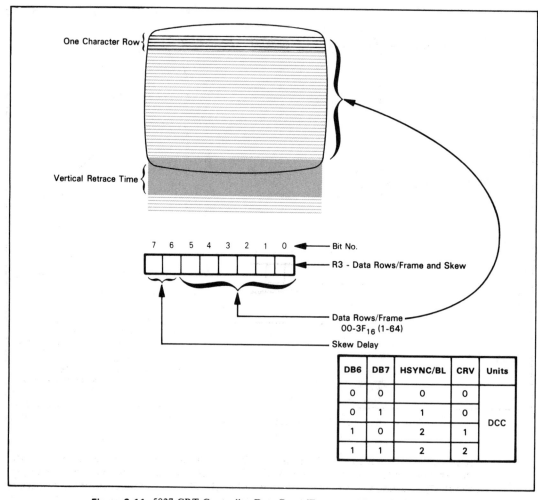

Figure 6-11. 5027 CRT Controller Data Rows/Frame and Skew Register (R3)

DB6	DB7	HSYNC/BL	CRV	Units
0	0	0	0	
0	1	1	0	
1	0	2	1	DCC
1	1	2	2	

Data Rows Per Frame and Skew Register (R3)

Figure 6-11 shows the format for the Data Rows Per Frame and Skew register (R3). **The six least significant bits determine the number of data rows that shall be displayed on the screen.** You can specify that from 1 to 64 rows be displayed. **The two most significant bits of register R3 allow you to specify that the HSYNC, BL, and CRV signals be delayed or skewed to account for the pipelining effect** that results from accumulated delays through character generator logic. Refer to Figure 6-7 to see the functional position of these delays in the CRT monitor interface.

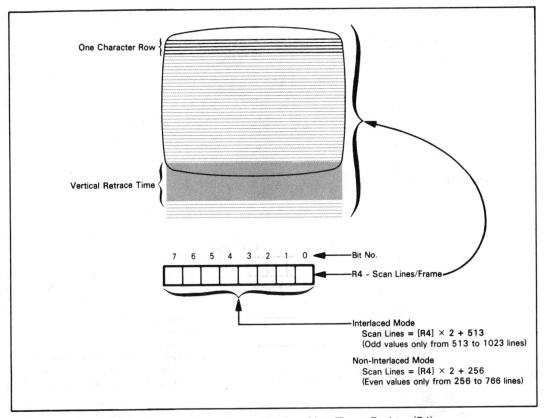

Figure 6-12. 5027 CRT Controller Scan Lines/Frame Register (R4)

Scan Lines Per Frame Register (R4)

Figure 6-12 shows the format for the Scan Lines Per Frame register (R4). As you can see in the figure, the way in which this register is programmed is dependent on whether the 5027 is operating in the interlaced or non-interlaced mode. In the interlaced mode, the total number of scan lines, including the time allowed for vertical retrace, is a minimum of 513, and a maximum of 1023 can be specified. In the interlaced mode, the number of scan lines specified must be an odd number. In the non-interlaced mode there can be from 256 to 766 scan lines per frame, and only even counts are permitted.

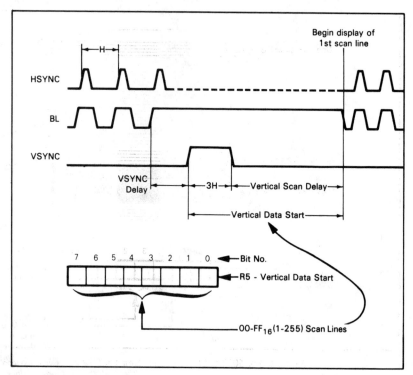

Figure 6-13. 5027 CRT Controller Vertical Data Start Register (R5)

Vertical Start Register (R5)

Figure 6-13 shows the format for the Vertical Start register (R5). This register defines the time, in scan lines, between the beginning of the VSYNC pulse and the beginning of display of the first scan line of the first data row on the screen. The duration of the VSYNC pulse itself is always equal to three scan line times. Thus, the vertical scan delay shown in Figure 6-13 is equal to the vertical start delay you specified minus 3 scan line times. One other delay is shown in Figure 6-13: VSYNC delay. This delay is not specified directly but can be derived by subtracting the vertical data start delay plus the total number of displayed scan lines per screen (see Register R3 and Register R2) from the total number of scan lines per frame (see Register R4).

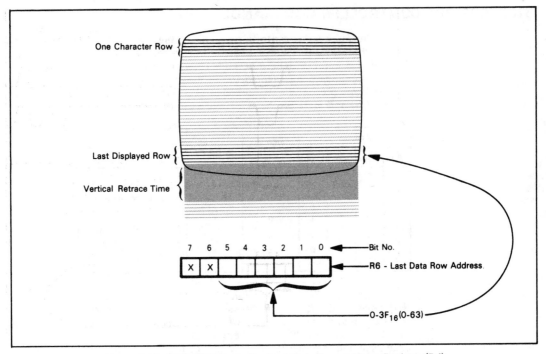

Figure 6-14. 5027 CRT Controller Last Data Row Address Register (R6)

Last Data Row Address Register (R6) Figure 6-14 shows the format for the Last Data Row Address register (R6). **This register defines the row address of the data that is to be displayed as the bottom row on the screen.** The function of this register should not be confused with that of Register R3, which defines the total number of displayed data rows per screen. **This register (R6) is associated with the scrolling function of the 5027.** For example, if you have defined that the screen is to display 24 data rows, then the top row on the screen would normally have a row address of 0 and the bottom row on the screen would be row 23. However, if you load Register R6 with the number 15, in this example, then the bottom row on the screen would have a row address of 15, the top row on the screen would be row 16, and rows 0 and 23 would be contiguous in the middle of the screen. Thus, Register R6 simply determines the row address that is to be output (on DR0-DR4) for the last displayed row on the screen and thus also determines the first row address that will be output after vertical retrace when the top row is being accessed from screen memory.

The 5027 also provides an Up Scroll command which simply increments the value held in R6 by 1. We will now proceed to describe the 5027 commands, including this Up Scroll command.

THE 5027 CRT CONTROLLER COMMANDS

The 5027 CRT controller provides nine different commands which were summarized in Table 6-1 earlier in this chapter. A portion of this table is expanded and reproduced here for reference purposes. As you will recall, these commands are issued in the same way that the control registers are accessed: you present the register address on inputs A0-A3 and apply the Chip Select (CS) and Data Strobe ($\overline{\text{DS}}$) signals to the 5027.

Address				Command Code (Hex)	Read (R) Write(W)	Command
A3	A2	A1	A0			
0	1	1	1	7	X	Processor-Initiated Self-Load
1	0	0	0	8	R	Read Cursor Row Address
1	0	0	1	9	R	Read Cursor Character (Column) Address
1	0	1	0	A	X	Reset
1	0	1	1	B	X	Up Scroll
1	1	0	0	C	W	Load Cursor Character (Column) Address
1	1	0	1	D	W	Load Cursor Row Address
1	1	1	0	E	X	Start Timing Chain
1	1	1	1	F	X	Non-Processor Self-Load

The two self-load commands are addressed as 7 (Processor Initiated Self-Load) and F_{16} (Non-Processor Self-Load). The operation of both of these commands was described when we discussed the 5027-microprocessor interface. The only difference between the two commands is the command code itself and the way that the commands terminate. The Processor-Initiated Self-Load command must be followed by the start timing chain command (E_{16}) to initiate operation of the 5027. The Non-Processor Self-Load command is terminated by removing the command code (F_{16}) from the A0-A3 inputs; this causes automatic initiatiation of 5027 operation.

There are four commands associated with the cursor position registers: command codes 8 and 9 read the contents of the cursor row address and cursor character or column address registers respectively, and command codes C_{16} and D_{16} are used to load the two cursor position registers. You will recall from our earlier discussion of the programmable registers that there are, in actuality, only two cursor position registers (the Row Address and Column Address registers), but that four addresses are required since there is no read/write input to the 5027. The Cursor Column address register is an 8-bit register, but only the six least significant bits of the Cursor Row Address register are used. Note that it is possible to load these cursor position registers with values which will be outside of the display area of the screen. For example, if you have specified that a data row is to be 80 characters wide and load the cursor column or character position register with a value greater than 80_{10}, then the cursor symbol would never be displayed. You must also remember that since the 5027 addresses screen memory on a row/column basis instead of on a linear basis, your software must keep track of where the end of a row is when it moves the cursor. You cannot simply continue to increment the Cursor Column Address register and cause the cursor to proceed to the next line on the display. Instead, when you reach the end of a row you must then increment the Row Address register to move the cursor to the next line.

The Reset command (A_{15}) causes the 5027 timing chain to be reset. The internal counters will be reset to values corresponding to the top left position of the screen. The Reset command is latched internally by the Data Strobe $(\overline{DS})$ signal and the counters will be held reset until you send the Start Timing Chain command to the 5027.

The Start Timing Chain command (E_{16}) must be used after a Reset or Processor-Initiated Self-Load command to allow the 5027 to resume operation. This command releases the timing chain approximately one scan-line time after it is received.

If you are using the microprocessor to initialize the 5027 by loading the control registers on startup rather than using one of the self-load modes, then a specific sequence of commands is required. The command sequence is as follows:

```
Start Timing Chain
Reset
Load Register 0
        .
        .
        .
Load Register 6
Start Timing Chain
```

While you must follow the sequence of START, RESET, LOAD, START to ensure proper initialization, it is not necessary to load the control registers in numerical order.

The Up Scroll command (B_{16}) simply causes the content of the Last Displayed Data Row register (R6) to be incremented by 1. This will cause the data displayed on the screen to be scrolled up one row with the former top line becoming the new bottom line on the screen. When the contents of R6 equals the contents of the lower 6 bits of R3 (Data Rows Per Frame register), R6 will be set to 0 when the next Up Scroll command is received. Thus your software need not worry about incrementing the contents of R6 to a value greater than the number of data rows on the screen; the 5027 automatically keeps the maximum value of R6 within the limits defined by R3.

THE 5027 CRT CONTROLLER TIMING CHAIN

Figure 6-15 illustrates the relationship between the programmable control registers of the 5027 and the generalized timing chain we developed in Chapter 1.

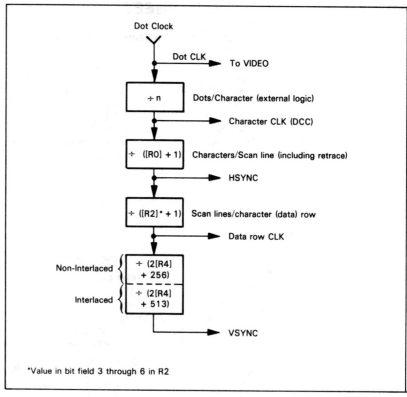

Figure 6-15. The Relationship between 5027 Programmable Registers
and the CRT Timing Chain

DATA SHEETS

This section contains specific electrical and timing data for the 5027.

5027

MAXIMUM GUARANTEED RATINGS*

Operating Temperature Range	0°C to + 70°C
Storage Temperature Range	−55°C to +150°C
Lead Temperature (soldering, 10 sec.)	+325°C
Positive Voltage on any Pin, with respect to ground	+18.0V
Negative Voltage on any Pin, with respect to ground	−0.3V

*Stresses above those listed may cause permanent damage to the device. This is a stress rating only and functional operation of the device at these or at any other condition above those indicated in the operational sections of this specification is not implied.

NOTE: When powering this device from laboratory or system power supplies, it is important that the Absolute Maximum Ratings not be exceeded or device failure can result. Some power supplies exhibit voltage spikes or "glitches" on their outputs when the AC power is switched on and off. In addition, voltage transients on the AC power line may appear on the DC output. For example, the bench power supply programmed to deliver +12 volts may have large voltage transients when the AC power is switched on and off. If this possibility exists it is suggested that a clamp circuit be used.

ELECTRICAL CHARACTERISTICS ($T_A = 0°C$ to 70°C, $V_{CC} = +5V \pm 5\%$, $V_{DD} = +12V \pm 5\%$, unless otherwise noted)

Parameter	Min.	Typ.	Max.	Unit	Comments
D.C. CHARACTERISTICS					
INPUT VOLTAGE LEVELS					
Low Level, V_{IL}			0.8	V	
High Level, V_{IH}	$V_{CC} - 1.5$		V_{CC}	V	
OUTPUT VOLTAGE LEVELS					
Low Level—V_{OL} for RØ-3			0.4	V	$I_{OL} = 3.2$ma
Low Level—V_{OL} all others			0.4	V	$I_{OL} = 1.6$ma
High Level—V_{OH} for RØ-3	2.4				$I_{OH} = 80\mu a$
High Level—V_{OH} all others	2.4				$I_{OH} = 40\mu a$
INPUT CURRENT					
Low Level, I_{IL}					
High Level, I_{IH}					
INPUT CAPACITANCE					
Data Bus, C_{IN}		10		pf	
Clock, C_{IN}		25		pf	
All other, C_{IN}		10		pf	
DATA BUS LEAKAGE in INPUT MODE					
I_{DB}					
I_{DB}					
POWER SUPPLY CURRENT					
I_{CC}		80		ma	
I_{DD}		40		ma	
A.C. CHARACTERISTICS					$T_A = 25°C$
DOT COUNTER CARRY					
frequency	0.2		4.0	MHz	Figure 1
PW_H	35			ns	Figure 1
PW_L	190			ns	Figure 1
tr, tf			10	ns	Figure 1
DATA STROBE					
$PW_{\overline{DS}}$		150		ns	Figure 2
ADDRESS, CHIP SELECT					
Set-up time		100		ns	Figure 2
Hold time		50		ns	Figure 2
DATA BUS—LOADING					
Set-up time		100		ns	Figure 2
Hold time		75		ns	Figure 2
DATA BUS—READING					
T_{DEL2}		100		ns	Figure 2, CL = 50pf
OUTPUTS: HØ-7, HS, VS, BL, CRV,					
CS-T_{DEL1}		100		ns	Figure 1, CL = 20pf
OUTPUTS: RØ-3, DRØ-5					
T_{DEL3}		1.0		μs	Figure 3, CL = 20pf

Restrictions

1. Only one pin is available for strobing data into the device via the data bus. The cursor X and Y coordinates are therefore loaded into the chip by presenting one set of addresses and outputed by presenting a different set of addresses. Therefore the standard WRITE and READ control signals from most microprocessors must be "NORed" externally to present a single strobe ($\overline{DS}$) signal to the device.

2. An even number of scan lines per character row must be programmed in interlace mode. This is again due to pin count limitations which require that the least significant bit of the scan counter serve as the odd/even field indicator.

3. In interlaced mode the total number of character slots assigned to the horizontal scan must be even to insure that vertical sync occurs precisely between horizontal sync pulses.

Data sheets on pages 6-26 and 6-27 are reprinted by permission of SMC Microsystems Corporation.

5027

AC TIMING DIAGRAMS

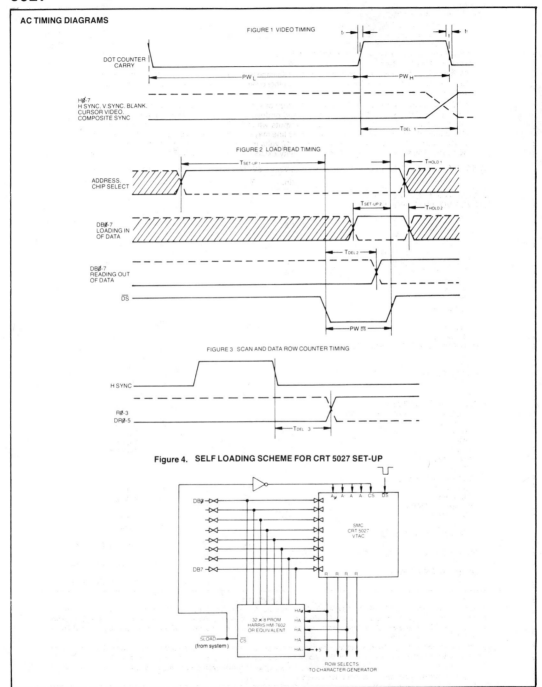

FIGURE 1 VIDEO TIMING

DOT COUNTER CARRY

H0-7
H SYNC, V SYNC, BLANK,
CURSOR VIDEO,
COMPOSITE SYNC

FIGURE 2 LOAD/READ TIMING

ADDRESS,
CHIP SELECT

DB0-7
LOADING IN
OF DATA

DB0-7
READING OUT
OF DATA

DS

FIGURE 3 SCAN AND DATA ROW COUNTER TIMING

H SYNC

R0-3
DR0-5

Figure 4. SELF LOADING SCHEME FOR CRT 5027 SET-UP

DB0

DB7

SMC
CRT 5027
VTAC

32 x 8 PROM
HARRIS HM 7602
OR EQUIVALENT

SLOAD
(from system)

ROW SELECTS
TO CHARACTER GENERATOR

Index

OSBORNE/McGraw-Hill GENERAL BOOKS

An Introduction to Microcomputers series
 by Adam Osborne
   Volume 0 — The Beginner's Book
   Volume 1 — Basic Concepts
   Volume 2 — Some Real Microprocessors (1978 ed.)
   Volume 3 — Some Real Support Devices (1978 ed.)
     Volume 2 1978-1979 Update Series
     Volume 3 1978-1979 Update Series

The 8089 I/O Processor Handbook
 by Adam Osborne
The 8086 Book
 by R. Rector and G. Alexy
8080 Programming for Logic Design
 by Adam Osborne
6800 Programming for Logic Design
 by Adam Osborne
Z80 Programming for Logic Design
 by Adam Osborne

8080A/8085 Assembly Language Programming
 by L. Leventhal
6800 Assembly Language Programming
 by L. Leventhal
Z80 Assembly Language Programming
 by L. Leventhal
6502 Assembly Language Programming
 by L. Leventhal
Z8000 Assembly Language Programming
 by L. Leventhal et al.
Running Wild: The Next Industrial Revolution
 by Adam Osborne
PET-CBM Personal Computer Guide
 by Carroll Donahue and Janice Enger
PET and the IEEE 488 Bus (GPIB)
 by E. Fisher and C. W. Jensen

OSBORNE/McGraw-Hill SOFTWARE

Practical Basic Programs
 by L. Poole et al.
Some Common BASIC Programs
 by L. Poole and M. Borchers
Some Common BASIC Programs PET Cassette
Some Common BASIC Programs PET Disk
Some Common BASIC Programs TRS-80 Cassette

Payroll with Cost Accounting - CBASIC
 by Lon Poole et al.
Accounts Payable and Accounts Receivable - CBASIC
 by Lon Poole et al.
General Ledger - CBASIC
 by Lon Poole et al.

Some Common Basic Programs — PET/CBM
 edited by Lon Poole et al.